Published by Awesome SA Publishers
info@awesomesa.co.za
Phone +27 (0)82 786 8450
www.awesomeSApublishers.co.za

Books are available in bulk to companies and organisations.
For more information, please contact the publisher.

First Edition September 2015

Printed and bound by ABC PRESS Cape Town

ISBN 978-0-620-65967-3 (soft cover)
ISBN 978-0-620-65968-0 (hard cover)

Whilst every effort has been made to ensure that the
information in this book was correct at the time of going
to press, details might since have changed. The author and
publishers accept no responsibility for any consequence,
loss, injury, damage or inconvenience sustained by any
person using this book as a reference.

The publisher apologises for any errors or omissions, and
would be grateful if notified of any corrections that should
be incorporated in future reprints or editions of this book.

Awesome SA Publishers

ABSOLUTELY AWESOME SOUTH AFRICA

Created by
Derryn Campbell

Art Direction
Kirsty Stirton

Editing
Brenda Daniels

Research & Proofreading
Brenda Daniels
Moray Comrie
Nicholas Challis
Daniella Toscana
Bronwen de Beer
Dee Vryenhoek
Nicole Graham
Jayme Wium

ABOUT THE BOOK

Living in South Africa is like riding a rollercoaster. When the ride commences, there is trepidation, however, this soon changes to exhiliration. The thrill of the experience and the view from the top is incredible and, in the end, you are left with a sense of accomplishment, wanting to go back for more.

That's how it is in South Africa. We live in a country with a vibrant economy, phenomenal people and breath-taking natural beauty. Whilst we have tremendous potential and a proven history of overcoming adversity, we are also confronted with many challenges which stir feelings of uncertainty. The purpose of this book is to remind us how far we have journeyed, of the spectacular beauty and how thrilling the experience of living in this country can be.

As with the first *Awesome South Africa* book, the information contained within will appeal to South Africans' two greatest attributes - their unwaivering pride and their awesome sense of humour. Many of the photographs or humorous anecdotes were taken from social media and I would like to thank the unknown originators for unwittingly sharing these.

I would like to express my gratitude towards the amazing people who contributed towards this book! In particular, to Brenda Daniels, Moray Comrie and Dee Vryenhoek, a very big thank you. To Kirsty Stirton, your captivating design of the entire book is fantastic and it has been a privilege to work with you. To my incredibly supportive family and friends, I could never have accomplished this book without your unrelenting encouragement, and lastly to Wayne, thank you for your belief in me - you are awesome!

I invite you to join me in embracing the awesomeness of the country that I am fortunate enough to call home.

Enjoy!

Derryn.

derryn@awesomesa.co.za

FOREWORD

If you read the newspaper headlines on any given day, you would think the country is on the brink of instant collapse. Listen to angry, noisy students on some of our campuses, and you could swear that a youthful revolution is about to hit the streets. Watch, in slow motion, the collapse of the major parastatals and you begin to wonder whether you should submit your tax returns to fund such incompetence. The negative stories have names - corruption, violence, racism, xenophobia, mismanagement, nepotism and many more.

All of these disasters happen, of course, but this is a small slice of the South African reality. There are more decent people than corrupt ones; hardworking citizens than lazy ones; ethical workers than thieves; honest neighbours than those seeking short-cuts to wealth and recognition by lying about their qualifications. How do I know this?

When I joined the University of the Free State more than six years ago, many of my friends thought of the job as a poisoned chalice. After the horrific incident called 'Reitz' (after the male residence where the atrocity occurred) in which white students racially humiliated black workers more than twice their ages, many believed the university would never recover from that crisis, and that black-white relations were irreversibly set back.

Nobody believes that anymore, at least not those who took the time to come through the campus and who observe the students as they live and learn together. While any institution that is more than 100 years old takes a long time to change deeply, and there is much still to do on the transformation journey, most agree that the UFS is a different place from its divided and bitter past.

There are two ways of looking at your reality - you can become depressed by focusing on the ample examples of dysfunction in our society or you can become hopeful by drawing on the many more instances of how 'awesome' people change their lot and that of others.

This is what I like about the publications of *Awesome South Africa* - these books provide real examples of great people, optimistic leaders, things we are proud of and, most importantly, lots of things to laugh about. We are, after all, a funny people; small wonder our main export is comedians.

Use this book as therapy, if you must, a resource to navigate around, through and above the day-to-day controversy that occupies the cocktail conversations. We are, after all, awesome!

Professor Jonathan Jansen

Professor Jonathan Jansen is the rector of the University of the Free State. He is the author of many books and, as an educationalist, holds an impressive collection of degrees and awards, including the position as President of the South African Institute of Race Relations.

CONTENTS

HAVING A LAUGH

HAVING A JOL 12
LEARN YOUR ABC 22
NOT FOR SISSIES 38
BY THE SEA 50
HAYIBO 80
DRIVING 88
TOYI TOYI 108
BLUNDERS 114
ROADSHOW 126
SHOPPING 146
NOW NOW 156
COMEDIANS 182
LOADSHEDDING 196
HARD DAY IN AFRICA 212
WILD ANIMALS 216

PUBLIC HOLIDAYS

HUMAN RIGHTS DAY 20
FREEDOM DAY 36
WORKERS' DAY 54
YOUTH DAY 72
WOMEN'S DAY 96
HERITAGE DAY 142
RECONCILIATION DAY 178

SPORTING NATION

SPORTING RECORDS 30
SPORT CAPTAINS 52
FISHING 90
QUIZ 110
CYCLING 152
ADVERSITY 170
SPORTING TRIVIA 190

Photo courtesy of Mohammed Alnaser

EVERYDAY LIVING

PLACE NAMES 34
MAKING BILTONG 62
COVER GIRLS 66
MENU ITEMS 74
WISE WORDS 100
UBUNTU GIRL 106
OUR FEAR 118
EMOTIONS 130
BEER OR WINE 132
THE BRAAI 162
HAVE A DRINK 184
MY SOUTH AFRICA 186
THE MAN I ENVY 200
FAVOURITE FOODS 202
WHAT KIDS SAY 206
INSPIRING THE WORLD 208
NATION THAT CARES 210
RAINBOW COLOURS 214

FACTS AND FIGURES

DID YOU KNOW? 16
WORLD RECORDS 60
SIGNS OF PROGRESS 70
HEALING PLANTS 82
UNIVERSITIES 86
TEST YOURSELF 128
POPULATION 138
PROVINCES 166
BUILDINGS 172
MONEY 174
HONOURS 176
DIAMONDS 192
INVENTIONS 194

WONDERS OF NATURE

TABLE MOUNTAIN 84
OUTER SPACE 120
CAMOUFLAGE 136
CONSERVATION 140
GREEN CANYON 144
THE LION KING 148
BARN SWALLOWS 158
RHINO POACHING 164
NATURAL DISASTERS 180

IN THE PAST

LONG WALK TO FREEDOM 14
THE LIFE OF MADIBA 26
BIRTHPLACE OF THE SUN 32
ANGLO-BOER WAR 42
TROUBLE STIRRERS 58
WHO THEY WERE 78
WORLD WAR 94
ROYALTY 98
SHIPWRECKS 112
SLAVE TRADE 116
GONDWANA LAND 122
APARTHEID EXPOSED 134
LEGENDARY JOURNEYS 150
POPULATION DESTROYERS 154
COULD IT BE TRUE? 198

CULTURE

NGUNI TRIBES 24
MUSIC GENRES 40
THE ANTHEM 44
LANGUAGES 46
THE KHOISAN 56
CUSTOMS 64
THE FLAG 76
RELIGION 92
LITERATURE 104
COAT OF ARMS 160
NATIONAL SYMBOLS 204

WORLD HERITAGE SITES

FLORAL KINGDOM 18
ROBBEN ISLAND 28
MAPUNGUBWE 48
VREDEFORT DOME 68
CRADLE OF HUMANKIND 102
RICHTERSVELD LANDSCAPE 124
ISIMANGALISO WETLAND PARK 168
MALOTI-DRAKENSBURG 188

Photo courtesy of Ayesha Cantor, Facebook, Africa, this is why I live here

HAVING A JOL!

Oxford Dictionary Definition:

Jol: (South African)

Noun: An occasion of celebration and enjoyment; a good time.
Verb: Have a good time; celebrate in a lively way.

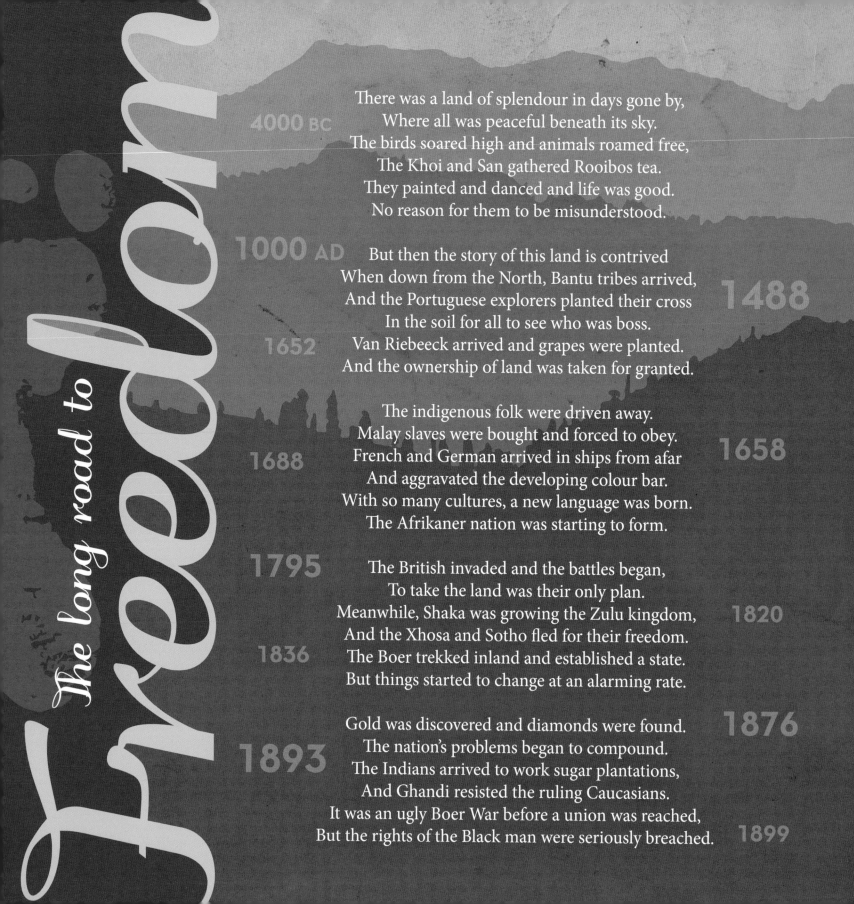

The long road to **Freedom**

4000 BC

There was a land of splendour in days gone by,
Where all was peaceful beneath its sky.
The birds soared high and animals roamed free,
The Khoi and San gathered Rooibos tea.
They painted and danced and life was good.
No reason for them to be misunderstood.

1000 AD

But then the story of this land is contrived
When down from the North, Bantu tribes arrived,
And the Portuguese explorers planted their cross
In the soil for all to see who was boss.
Van Riebeeck arrived and grapes were planted.
And the ownership of land was taken for granted.

1488

1652

The indigenous folk were driven away.
Malay slaves were bought and forced to obey.
French and German arrived in ships from afar
And aggravated the developing colour bar.
With so many cultures, a new language was born.
The Afrikaner nation was starting to form.

1688

1658

The British invaded and the battles began,
To take the land was their only plan.
Meanwhile, Shaka was growing the Zulu kingdom,
And the Xhosa and Sotho fled for their freedom.
The Boer trekked inland and established a state.
But things started to change at an alarming rate.

1795

1820

1836

Gold was discovered and diamonds were found.
The nation's problems began to compound.
The Indians arrived to work sugar plantations,
And Ghandi resisted the ruling Caucasians.
It was an ugly Boer War before a union was reached,
But the rights of the Black man were seriously breached.

1876

1893

1899

A dark time for all, the future foreboding.
Segregation worsening, and hatred growing.
The terms of apartheid were forced on the land.
The ANC was formed and subsequently banned.
The oppressed revolted and then were imprisoned.
But the government was feeling increasingly threatened.

There were rumblings of change, the people were scared.
'Will it ever work if rights are shared?'
The government finally came to its senses,
And allowed the Black man to cross the fences.
Mandela was freed and led the nation,
Into a time of peace and celebration.

The people soon realised there was work to be done,
That required full commitment from everyone.
There were bridges to build, and wounds to heal,
To learn love and respect in a way that was real.
All agreed that we faced a long road ahead,
And remembered the words of Mandela who said:

1910
1948
1960
1980
1989
1992
1994
2000s

'I have walked that long road to freedom. I have tried not to falter; I have made missteps along the way. But I have discovered the secret that after climbing a great hill, one only finds that there are many more hills to climb. I have taken a moment here to rest, to steal a view of the glorious vista that surrounds me, to look back on the distance I have come. But I can rest only for a moment, for with freedom comes responsibilities, and I dare not linger, for my long walk is not yet ended.'

BEFORE GOOGLE WE HAD CHAPPIES IN SOUTH AFRICA

DID YOU KNOW?
CHAPPIES BUBBLEGUM IS A SOUTH AFRICAN FAVOURITE. IN THE PAST IT WAS SOLD FOR 1/2 CENT EACH, AND WAS OFTEN GIVEN AS CHANGE!

DID YOU KNOW?
PATRICE MOTSEPE, SOUTH AFRICA'S MINING MAGNATE, IS LISTED AMONG THE TOP 10 RICHEST BLACK PEOPLE IN THE WORLD FOR 2015

DID YOU KNOW?
IN 1882 KIMBERLEY WAS THE FIRST CITY IN THE SOUTHERN HEMISPHERE TO INSTALL ELECTRIC STREET LIGHTING. AT THIS TIME, LONDON STILL RELIED ON GAS LAMPS FOR STREET LIGHTING

DID YOU KNOW?
SOUTH AFRICA IS ONE OF THE TOP 10 COUNTRIES IN THE WORLD HARNESSING RENEWABLE ENERGY FROM THE SUN

DID YOU KNOW?
THE 6 000 YEAR OLD BAOBAB TREE IN LIMPOPO PROVINCE HAS A HOLLOWED-OUT TRUNK WHICH HAS BEEN CONVERTED INTO A BAR THAT CAN HOLD OVER 60 PEOPLE

DID YOU KNOW?
THE HOTTEST TEMPERATURE EVER RECORDED IN SOUTH AFRICA WAS 50° C IN DUNBRODY IN THE EASTERN CAPE

DID YOU KNOW?
SOUTH AFRICA'S CONSTITUTION IS THE FIRST IN THE WORLD TO GUARANTEE EQUALITY FOR GAY AND LESBIAN PEOPLE

DID YOU KNOW?
SOUTH AFRICA HAS THE SECOND-OLDEST FILM INDUSTRY IN THE WORLD

DID YOU KNOW?
THE ARCH AT THE MOSES MABHIDA STADIUM IS 106 M HIGH, MAKING IT HIGHER THAN THE STATUE OF LIBERTY IN NEW YORK

DID YOU KNOW?
THE OLDEST SOUTH AFRICAN BRAND NAME, FOUNDED IN 1685, IS GROOT CONSTANTIA

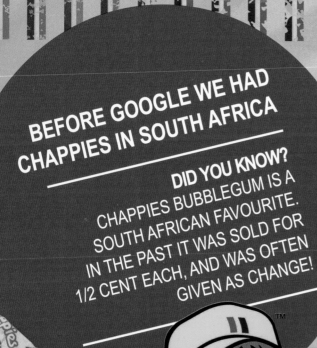

DID YOU KNOW?
OVER 500 WEBSITES LIST MOSSEL BAY AS HAVING THE MILDEST CLIMATE IN THE WORLD, SECOND ONLY TO HAWAII

DID YOU KNOW?
A ZAMBEZI SHARK IS KNOWN TO TOLERATE FRESH WATER AND WAS CAUGHT IN THE KRUGER NATIONAL PARK ABOUT 200 KM FROM THE SEA

DID YOU KNOW?
PAUL KRUGER, THE SOUTH AFRICAN PRESIDENT FROM 1883 BELIEVED THAT THE WORLD WAS FLAT

DID YOU KNOW?
IN 1960 A BYLAW IN DURBAN WAS CHANGED ALLOWING BIKINIS TO BE WORN ON THE BEACHES

DID YOU KNOW?
COMPUTICKET WAS THE WORLD'S FIRST COMPUTERISED ENTERTAINMENT BOOKING SYSTEM

DID YOU KNOW?
THE TUGELA WATER FALLS IN THE DRAKENSBERG ARE THE SECOND HIGHEST IN THE WORLD

DID YOU KNOW?
BEFORE IT WAS CLOSED IN 1935, THE DURBAN BLUFF WAS HOME TO THE LARGEST LAND-BASED WHALING OPERATION IN THE WORLD

DID YOU KNOW?
UKHOZI FM IS THE SECOND-BIGGEST RADIO STATION IN THE WORLD WITH A LISTENERSHIP OF OVER 6.5 MILLION PEOPLE

DID YOU KNOW?
IT TAKES ONE MINUTE LONGER TO BOIL AN EGG IN JOHANNESBURG THAN IT DOES AT THE COASTAL CITY OF DURBAN

DID YOU KNOW?
WERE YOU TO BURROW DOWN FROM DURBAN, THROUGH THE CENTRE OF THE EARTH YOU WOULD POP UP AT KAHULUI, MAUI, HAWAII

DID YOU KNOW?
AARDVARK IS THE FIRST ENTRY IN MOST *ENGLISH* DICTIONARIES

DID YOU KNOW?
THE CHRIS HANI BARAGWANATH HOSPITAL IS THE LARGEST ACUTE HOSPITAL IN THE WORLD

DID YOU KNOW?
THE TEST KITCHEN IN CAPE TOWN IS INCLUDED IN THE WORLD'S 50 BEST RESTAURANTS FOR 2015

Did you know?

Flower Safari

when the west coast area explodes like fireworks into fields of colour

Unesco's World Heritage Committee declared the 553 000-hectare Cape Floral Region to be of 'outstanding universal significance to humanity', describing it as 'one of the richest areas for plants in the world'.

Photo courtesy Marna Cilliers, Green Vision Foundation

The Cape Floral kingdom is one of eight world heritage sites in South Africa.

This is the smallest yet richest of the six floral kingdoms in the world.

Ten per cent of the world's flowering species are found in South Africa.

The flower species include the unique Fynbos and Renosterveld vegetation.

South Africa is the only country in the world with an entire plant kingdom inside our borders.

The Cape Floral Kingdom stretches from Cape Point to Grahamstown and up to the Southern Cape's Olifants River.

This is also one of the biodiversity hotspots on Earth as almost 70 % of all the plant species are endemic and only found within our borders.

South Africa is home to the world's smallest succulent plants (less than 9.9 mm) and the largest (the baobab tree, around 20 m tall).

The Cape Floral Region contains more plant species per square metre than anywhere else on our planet.

Cape Floral Region, Western Cape

UNESCO

Human Rights Day

Human Rights Day is a day of celebration. It celebrates the country's Bill of Rights, the foundation of South Africa's democracy, and emphasises the human dignity, equality and freedom of **all** South Africans. That Human Rights Day is a celebration is no small wonder, considering this country's apartheid past. Rights abuses suffered by Black people during those years included restriction of freedom of expression, of association and of movement and residence. In fact, Black people were forced to carry passbooks or special identification documents. While White counterparts were not required to carry passes, Black people could be fined or imprisoned if found without these papers.

When Black people in Sharpeville, Gauteng, organised a demonstration on 21 March 1960 against the pass laws, carnage resulted. What is known today as the Sharpeville massacre led to the deaths of 69 demonstrators and the injury of a further 186. Over 50 years later it is indeed wonderful that we **celebrate** the 21st of March; human rights for all are now exalted, not violated!

South Africa's Constitution is regarded as one of the most progressive in the world. Its adoption was a long process, beginning in 1990 with the unbanning of political parties and culminating with approval on 4 December 1996. The Bill of Rights forms one of the 14 chapters of the Constitution. South Africa is governed according to this Constitution; it is the highest law in the land.

We, the people of South Africa, recognise the injustices of our past; Honour those who suffered for justice and freedom in our land; Respect those who have worked to build and develop our country; and Believe that South Africa belongs to all who live in it, united in our diversity.

- From the Preamble to the Constitution of South Africa

Bill of Rights

The Bill of Rights is a cornerstone of democracy in South Africa. It enshrines the rights of all people in this country and affirms the democratic values of human dignity, equality and freedom. The state must respect, protect, promote and fulfil the rights in the Bill of Rights. The Bill of Rights applies to all law, and binds the legislature, the executive, the judiciary and all organs of state. The rights in the Bill, among others, include:

- Everyone has a basic human dignity which must be respected. You cannot be discriminated against.

- Everyone has the right to life.

- You have the right to use the language of your choice and practise your own culture.

- You have the right to a basic education in the official language of your choice.

- Your right to privacy includes your body, home and possessions.

- When arrested, you have the right to remain silent, to be brought before a court within 48 hours, and the right to legal representation.

- You have the right to think, believe and worship however you may choose.

- You have the right to resolve legal disputes in a court or another impartial tribunal.

- You have the right to form, join and maintain cultural, linguistic and religious groupings of your own choice.

Did you know?

A cracked and aged section of wall of the Old Durban Central Prison stands today adjacent to the Inkosi Albert Luthuli International Convention Centre in Durban. The prison has a dark history of human rights violations. The remaining wall was painted in 1992 with a colourful mural to celebrate human rights associated with the freedom struggle. A visit to the wall (pictured) is a constant reminder of the human rights of each individual South African.

...ABC my way

A is for **Aikona!** - 'no never' we cry. **B** is for **babbelaas** - too much drink at the braai.

C is for **CHOW** - food fit for a King. **D** is for **dinges** - to explain 'that thing'.

E is for **eina** - when it hurts really sore. **F** is for **fundi** - the one who knows more.

G is for **GOGOS** - the grannies we love, **H** is for **hadeda** - our South African dove.

I is for **izit** - when saying 'is that so?' **J** is for **JOL** - a good party we know!

K is for **kaalgat** - if you dare to go bare, **L** is for **lekker** - a tasty affair.

M is for **moegoe** - a fool in his prime, **N** is for **NOW NOW** - we're on African time!

O is for **oke** - that dude over there, **P** is for **PAS OP** - you had better beware.

Q is for **quarter bunny** - Durban's favourite meal, **R** is for **rock up** - so pitch when you feel.

S is for **sies** - when it's really not nice, **T** is for **tune** - when we give you advice.

U is for **ubuntu** - compassionate and kind, **V** is for **voetsek** - not for dogs or mankind.

W is for **walkie talkies** - chicken feet and the beak,

X is for **Xhosa** - who 'click' when they speak.

Y is for **YEBO** - a definite yes, **Z** is for **zebra** - in spectacular dress.

Arrival of the
NGUNI
-TRIBES-

THE MIGRATION TOWARDS SOUTHERN AFRICA

Sometime, over 5000 years ago, the ancestral speakers of modern Bantu languages broke away from West Africa and moved eastwards and southwards. The easternmost group split into two - the Sotho-Tswana and the Nguni.

The migration of the Nguni occurred in waves over many centuries. According to legend, sometime between the 2nd and 5th centuries, the Nguni people migrated southwards with large herds of cattle, expanding across sub-Saharan Africa into Southern Africa. Along the way groups split off: the Swazi to the north, the Zulu towards the east and the Xhosa to the south.

Owing to the fact that the Swazi, Xhosa and Zulu had a common origin, their languages and cultures show marked similarities. Prior to the arrival of the Nguni, the San were the only indigenous people in what is today known as South Africa. At some point along their southward journey, the Nguni came in contact with San hunters. This contact influenced the Nguni languages resulting in the 'click' sounds which characterise their languages today.

THE MFECANE

By the early 1800s the Nguni had established themselves into divided political entities, each with their own chiefs who had both political and ritual powers. Then a massive tragedy struck in a period of wars and resettlement. This period is referred to by the Nguni as 'the Mfecane' ('the crushing') and by the Sotho-Tswana as 'Difaqane' ('the scattering of tribes'). At this time a long drought had made most of Southern Africa inhospitable and different tribes fought over scarce resources. Over two million people wandered about seeking food and shelter, and the Highveld region occupied by the Sotho-Tswana people was in disarray. This general confusion led to the rise of Shaka Zulu in 1815. In two decades Shaka created an expansive Zulu state. His powerful army waged war on neighbouring peoples causing them to be incorporated into the Zulu state or to flee as refugees. These refugees, copying the new military discipline and the strategy developed by Shaka, were able to conquer other African peoples and to establish new states throughout Southern and Central Africa. These included the Ndebele who expanded northwards under the leadership of Mzilikazi, and the Swazi who developed into present-day Swaziland under Chief Sobhuza.

Wars between the Nguni people and the Europeans further impacted on the Nguni people. Slowly, over time, they were conquered by the expanding European power. A large number of the Nguni men were forced to become migrant labourers throughout Southern Africa. This process was accelerated sharply in the period after 1886 when large gold deposits were discovered in the Witwatersrand.

TODAY ...

It is more difficult to isolate the Nguni people in modern-day South Africa. You will, however, find communities who practise the traditional Nguni customs in the rural areas of the Eastern Cape, Kwazulu-Natal and Mpumalanga. These include the Swazi, Zulu, Ndebele and the Xhosa.

From the Nguni people emerged four of South Africa's official languages. These languages are often mutually intelligible. The majority of the Nguni-language group – isiZulu, isiXhosa and siSwati, for example – have adopted a variety of hybrid and cosmopolitan lifestyles and today the term 'Nguni' is used in a linguistic sense as opposed to once being used to describe a group of people.

THE ABUNDANT HERDS

The Nguni cattle have been present in Africa for about 8000 years. Cattle have always played a vital role in Nguni society in which a man's importance was measured by the size of his herd. The Nguni migrated with their cattle from East Africa, after which the cattle were interbred with European types to produce the modern hides of striking variety in colour and pattern. This gave rise to an equally colourful practice of describing the hides of the Nguni cattle, resulting in over 350 isiXhosa or isiZulu words for this purpose.

The Nguni cattle have become South Africa's indigenous cattle. They enjoy natural grazing and are ideally suited to the harsh African climate. They can survive in both hot and cold climates and have a strong immune system which is resistant to numerous diseases.

MANDELA

Photo © Duncan Hull

Mr Nelson Rolihlahla Mandela: is referred to by many names, each with its own special meaning and story...

NELSON - the name given to him on his first day at school by his teacher, Miss Mdingane.

ROLIHLAHLA - his birth name, the colloquial isiXhosa meaning 'troublemaker'.

MANDELA - his family surname.

MADIBA - This is his clan name and refers to his ancestor. Madiba was the name of a Thembu chief who ruled in the Transkei in the 18th century.

TATA - An isiXhosa term of endearment meaning 'father' as he was a father figure to many.

NUMBER 466/64 - the number assigned to him whilst in prison on Robben Island.

ROBBEN ISLAND PRISON INMATES:
Walter Sisulu, Ahmed Kathrada, Raymond Mhlaba, Govan Mbeki, Elias Motsoaledi, and Andrew Mlangeni. Denis Goldberg was also convicted but sent to Pretoria because he was White.

THE LIFE OF AN INSPIRATION AND ICON

1918	Born at Mvezo in the Transkei on July 18
1934	Undergoes initiation; Attends Clarkebury Boarding Institute in Engcobo
1937	Attends Healdtown College at Fort Beaufort
1939	Enrols at the University College of Fort Hare, in Alice
1940	Expelled from the University of Fort Hare
1942	Completes BA through the University of South Africa
1942	Informally attends African National Congress meetings

1943	Enrols for an LLB at Wits University
1944	Co-founds the ANC Youth League (ANCYL)
1948	Elected national secretary of the ANCYL
1951	Elected President of the ANCYL
1952	Defiance Campaign begins. Convicted with Sisulu and 17 others for violating the Suppression of Communism Act; sentenced to nine months' imprisonment, suspended for two years; elected first of ANC deputy presidents; opens South Africa's first Black law firm with Oliver Tambo

Mandela's Wives:

Evelyn Ntoko Mase: married 1944 – 1958. They had two daughters and two sons: Thembikile, Makaziwe, Makgatho, Makaziwe (his first daughter Makaziwe died in infancy and his second daughter was named in her honour).

Nomzamo Winnie Madikizela: married 1958 - 1996. They had two daughters: Zenani and Zindziswa.

Graca Machel: married in 1998 on his 80th birthday.

Nelson Mandela International Day

It is more than a celebration of Madiba's life and legacy. It is a global movement to honour his life's work and to act to change the world for the better.

The day was launched in recognition of Nelson Mandela's birthday on **18 July 2009** by a unanimous decision of the UN General Assembly.

It was inspired by a call Nelson Mandela made a year earlier for the next generation to take on the burden of leadership in addressing the world's social injustices; he said: 'It is in your hands now.'

Did You Know?

Mandela was arrested on several occasions and stood trial four times.

???

Mandela declined an offer from PW Botha in 1985 for conditional release from prison because he was not prepared to renounce violence and violent protest as a means to bring about change in South Africa.

Madiba Inauguration Speech (1994)

We understand it still that there is no easy road to freedom. We know it well that none of us acting alone can achieve success. We must therefore act together as a united people, for national reconciliation, for nation building, for the birth of a new world. Let there be justice for all. Let there be peace for all. Let there be work, bread, water and salt for all. Let them know that for each the body, the mind and the soul have been freed to fulfil themselves. Never, never and never again shall it be that this beautiful land will again experience the oppression of one by another and suffer the indignity of being the skunk of the world. Let freedom reign. The sun shall never set on so glorious a human achievement. God bless Africa!

Mandela portraits courtesy of the Pietermaritzburg community

1953	Devises the M-Plan for the ANC's underground operations
1956	Arrested for treason with 155 others; all are acquitted
1960	A State of Emergency imposed; the ANC is banned
1961	Goes underground; Umkhonto weSizwe is formed
1962	Leaves the country for military training; returns to report back to ANC president Chief Albert Luthuli; arrested in KwaZulu-Natal and sentenced to five years for incitement and for leaving the country illegally
1963	Sent to Robben Island; returned with nine others to Pretoria for the Rivonia sabotage trial
1964	Makes his famous speech from the dock in which he says he is 'prepared to die' for a democratic South Africa
1982	Transferred with others to Pollsmoor Prison
1985	Rejects president PW Botha's offer to release him if he renounces violence
1986	Begins talks about talks between the National Party government and the ANC
1988	Hospitalised for tuberculosis then moved to Victor Verster Prison
1989	Meets PW Botha; then Botha's successor FW de Klerk; graduates with an LLB from Unisa
1990	President De Klerk unbans all political organisations; released from prison
1993	Awarded the Nobel Peace Prize with De Klerk
1994	Elected as president
1999	Steps down after one term as president
2004	Announces he is stepping down from public life
2008	Celebrates his 90th birthday
2013	Dies on December 5, at the age of 95

Robben Island

The island in Table Bay is 5 km^2 and lies 7 km from Cape Town. Its name 'robben' is derived from the Dutch, meaning 'a seal'.

The island is notorious for its sad and harsh history and has become a symbol of the strength of the human spirit. The island represents freedom and the victory of democracy over oppression.

Photo courtesy of Marna Cilliers, Green Vision Foundation

1488 In 1488 Bartholomeu Dias anchors in Table Bay and discovers the island. In the course of time the Portuguese set up a station on the island to replenish their supplies of fresh water and meat. Sheep are introduced and a mail station is set up. On occasion, seafarers take refuge there when there are clashes with the indigenous people on the mainland.

1652 Van Riebeeck, in addition to the refuelling station for ships, uses the island as a convict station for criminals. The prisoners included kings, princes and religious leaders from the East Indies who did not agree with the Dutch rule in their country.

1806 When the British annex the Cape, they continue the practice of a convict station but also build a whaling station on the island. However, when it becomes apparent that it offers convicts an easy escape route, the whaling station is closed down in 1820.

1843 The island is used as a medical infirmary and becomes the home for the Colony's unwanted and unloved, those deemed to be 'mentally ill', which includes the homeless, alcoholics, those too sick or old to work, and prostitutes with sexually transmitted diseases. By 1893, the island is used specifically as a leper colony.

1913 The mental patients from the island are integrated into more humane institutions of care on the mainland and the island becomes a military outpost before WW II. Guns are stored there and the government builds roads, a power station, a new water supply and houses.

1960 Construction of the maximum security prison of the apartheid period begins. Political activists like Nelson Mandela are imprisoned on the island.

1997 After four centuries of imprisonment and banishment, the Robben Island Museum is opened and thereafter declared a World Heritage Site.

Robben Island, Western Cape

GLOBAL CONTENDERS

Transcending race and language groups, sport unites the country. There are too many record breakers to mention. These are just a handful of champions that have inspired the nation.

BLACK KNIGHT

GARY PLAYER has nine major wins on the regular PGA Tour and nine on the senior PGA Tour. He was the only winner of the Grand Slam on both the regular and the senior tours. His numerous accolades include being the first international recipient of the PGA Tour's Lifetime Achievement Award and the Laureus Lifetime Achievement Award for dedication to charity.

NIGHTWATCHMAN

MARK BOUCHER, with 999 dismissals, holds the world record for the most international dismissals by a wicketkeeper. He has completed the unique Test double of 5000 runs and 500 dismissals. He is the only wicketkeeper to score a 50 and effect six dismissals in a Test match innings twice.

THE MIDMAR MILE

With 13 755 swimmers, the event is listed in the Guinness Book of World Records as the world's largest open water swim. The event originated in 1974 when three friends, who were unable to compete in the Buffalo Mile in East London because of petrol restrictions, decided to stage their own race in KwaZulu-Natal.

ROSE OF SOWETO

DINGAAN THOBELA held the World Boxing Organisation's lightweight title which he defended on two occasions. When he won the WBC Super Middleweight title, he was the first South African to win a WBC belt in his home country. He would hand out roses to beautiful girls at the ringside, earning him the name 'Rose of Soweto'.

INSPIRATION

ZANELE SITU broke the Paralympic world record for javelin to become the first Black South African to win a Paralympic gold medal. She received the Whang Youn Dai Achievement Award, which is presented to a male or female athlete who best exemplifies the spirit of the Games and inspires and excites the world.

GOLDEN BOY

JOSIAH THUGWANE became the first Black South African athlete to have won an Olympic gold medal. This was despite being shot and injured during a hijacking five months before the Olympics. His successes include winning the Nagano Marathon in Japan and the largest half marathon in the world, the UK's Great North Run.

BREASTSTROKE QUEEN

PENNY HEYNS was the first South African to win gold in 44 years. She became the only woman in Olympic history to win both the 100 m and 200 m breaststroke events. She set 14 individual breaststroke world records, more than any other male or female swimmer in history and the only one to hold world records in all three breaststroke distances.

DUSI CANOE MARATHON

This, the biggest canoeing event on the African continent, and one of the world's most popular river marathons, attracts between 1600 and 2000 paddlers each year. The event was born during World War II when Ian Player, sitting around a campfire in Italy, came up with the idea to race from Pietermaritzburg to Durban.

UNSUNG HERO

JACQUES KALLIS is the only cricketer in history to have scored over 11 000 runs and taken 250 wickets in both ODIs and Tests. Kallis topped the ICC rankings several times and was awarded ICC Cricketer of the Year and ICC Test Player of the Year. He is listed in the top five Test all-rounders.

POLLY PERFECTION

SHAUN POLLOCK, who captained the Proteas, was the most economical bowler in the world and third on the ICC player rankings for all-time best ODI bowlers.

LOOP EN VAL

MATTHEWS MOTSHWARATEU, whose nickname meant 'Walk-and-Fall' because of his awkward style of running, became the first black South African to break a world record when he ran the 10 km road race in New York in 1980. Despite his running style, he became one of the world's greatest cross county and track athletes.

THE ROCKET

ROLAND SCHOEMAN is the fastest man over the 50 m freestyle. He is a three time Olympic medal winner and nine-time world record holder.

UNBELIEVABLE

CHAD LE CLOS became the youngest-ever world champion at the age of 18 when he won the 200 m butterfly and went on to break his own short-course world record. His list of gold medals is still growing and he has been awarded the overall World Cup series winner more than once.

ULTIMATE SPRINGBOK

FRIK DU PREEZ, known as the 'Ultimate Springbok', was voted South African Rugby player of the 20th century. There were two South Africans included when the IRB's Rugby Hall of Fame was introduced in 1997; they were Danie Craven and Frik du Preez.

SOWETO DERBY

The fierce rivalry between Premier Soccer League's Kaizer Chiefs and Orlando Pirates is broadcast globally to over 100 million households around the world. This colourful and joyous event is known as the 'Soweto Derby'. It is one of the most fiercely contested matches in African football.

PRINCE OF BIG AIR

GREG MINNAAR, downhill mountain bike racer, is the three-times Downhill World Champion with 18 Downhill World Cup victories and 64 Downhill World Cup podiums. He has been appointed a member of the renowned International Cycling Union's (UCI) Athlete Commission.

THE BIG O

OSCAR CHALUPSKY is a 12-time world surfski champion. He won his first Molokai world challenge at the age of 20 and when he won his twelfth championship he was 49 years old, making him the only person to have won the race in three different decades.

WORLD'S BEST

HESTRIE CLOETE, winner of numerous gold medals, was voted the world's best performer and crowned IAAF World Athlete of the Year. She became the world's number-one high jumper and the first woman high jumper to successfully defend her World Championship title.

THE BIRTHPLACE OF THE SUN

THE STONE CIRCLES

The mystifying discoveries of the thousands of stone circle ruins in Mpumalanga boggles the imagination. Their existence challenges accepted belief and creates much debate about their origin and purpose.

Were the Stone Circles built by a Lost Civilisation?

A vast network of man-made stone walling forms a complex maze of circular structures, terraced fields and linking roads. It is estimated that these structures stretch for 150 km in an almost continuous belt covering an area of over 10 000 km². In some cases the walls of the structures are as much as 2.5 m high. The extremely hard hornfels stones used to construct the stone circles have an acoustic nature and are able to be rung like bells. Also significant is the presence of hundreds of ancient gold mines in close proximity to the ruins and indication points towards a civilisation which mined gold.

An ancient road structure is evident which connects all the ruins indicating a well-planned and evolved civilization. Extensive agricultural terraces are spread over large areas, often resembling scenes from the Inca settlements in Peru. Many of the circular structures are aligned to specific geographic points as well as with solstices and equinoxes.

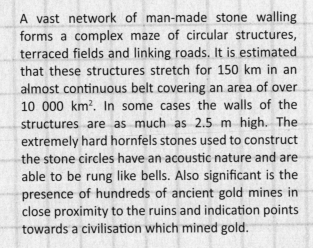

Could these ancient settlements actually be the lost kingdom of Queen Sheba and the mines that provided King Solomon with all his riches?

Did the Egyptians, Incas and Phoenicians visit the area?

Oral traditions have named the area Bokoni - the country of the Koni people who date back to between 1500 and 1820. Archeologists are divided about whether the Koni themselves developed the infrastructure or whether they inherited the structures from previous civilisations.

Various tools and artefacts that have been recovered from these ruins show a long and extended period of settlement. It is claimed by some that many of these artefacts show that virtually every ancient culture was present here in southern Africa at some point in history. This includes the Sumerians, Egyptians, Phoenicians, Romans, Greeks, Arabs, Dogon, Dravidians, and even the Incas.

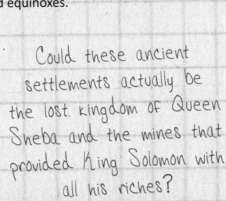

ADAM'S CALENDAR

The mystery of the Stone Circles culminates in a ring of stones known as Adam's Calendar. This spectacular ancient site is aligned with the N,S,E,W cardinal points of the Earth and marks the solstices and equinoxes. The stones are still accurate as a calendar by following the shadow of the setting sun, which is cast by the taller central monolith onto the flat calendar stone beside it.

The calendar provides insight into African societies' understanding of the sun's movement. Based on a number of scientific evaluations, it has been dated to be at least 75 000 years of age.

How did this ancient people understand the sun's movements to accurately mark the solstices and the equinoxes?

The site is built along the same longitudinal line as the Great Zimbabwe Ruins and the Great Pyramid of Giza in Egypt, suggesting a connection between those ancient civilisations and the builders of all three of these sites. Despite scepticism of the theories on the circles, there is little doubt that the recently re-discovered Adam's Calendar is of important historical and cultural significance.

The calendar was re-discovered in 2003 by Johan Heine and named by Michael Tellinger as Adam's Calendar because it is possibly the oldest structure on Earth that is linked to human origins. It has, however, been known by African elders, indigenous knowledge keepers and shamans as 'The Birthplace of The Sun', or *'Inzalo y'Langa'* where humanity was created by the gods.

Who built the calendar that lines up with the Great Pyramids of Giza in Egypt and the Great Zimbabwe ruins?

Could this be the oldest structure on Earth linked to humans?

THE STONE RUINS
IN MPUMALANGA

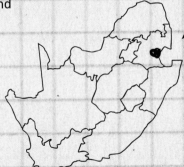

Book an interesting tour of the Stone Circles though Stone Circle Bistro and Backpackers, www.michaeltellinger.com/stonecircle

THE NAMING GAME

PARTS OF A WHOLE

... baai (bay) as in Gansbaai
... vlei (marsh) as in Verlorenvlei
... berg (mountain) as in Muizenberg
... burg (fort/castle) as in Middelburg
... stroom (stream) as in Dullstroom
... kop (head) as in Klapmutskop
... kwa (place of) as in KwaMashu
... dorp (town) as in Humansdorp
... bosch (bush) as in Rondebosch
... fontein (fountain) as in Bloemfontein
... spruit (water course) as in Nelspruit
... poort (narrow pass) as in Komatipoort
... kloof (gorge) as in Waterkloof
... hoek (corner) as in Franschoek

NYLSTROOM - translated to Nile River, got its name after a renowned religious cult, the Jerusalem Trekkers, were on their way to Egypt and when coming across a river filled with reeds and crocodile, mistook it for the 'Nile River'. In addition to the river they saw a hill vaguely like a pyramid, which is why they thought they had reached Egypt. Nylstroom was renamed Modimolle which means 'the forefather's spirit has eaten' (Modimo o Ile). The story goes that its people would sometimes climb the mountain, only to disappear without trace. The Sotho people attributed such disappearances to 'an ancestral spirit that ate (killed) the unfortunate.'

FINDING MEANING

SOWETO – The infamous township lies southwest of Johannesburg. Its name is formed from the first letters of 'South Western Township'.

GAUTENG – Meaning 'Place of Gold' in Sotho because of its gold mining heritage.

MPUMALANGA – Meaning 'Place of the Rising Sun,' it was named in 1993 to pay tribute to the dawning of a new democratic South Africa.

KWAZULU-NATAL - 'KwaZulu' means 'place of the Zulu people'. 'Natal' is Portuguese for 'Christmas' and was given by the Portuguese sailors to the coast that they reached on Christmas Day of 1497.

NOW THAT'S A MOUTHFUL!

Gingindlovu
Kromellenboogspruit
Ntabakayaikhonjwa
Seweweekspoort
Tsitsikamma
Ystervarkpunt
Phuthaditjhaba
Thabazimbi

With 44 letters, this small farm in South Africa holds the record for the longest official one-word place name in Africa. Literally it translates to 'two buffaloes shot dead using one shot fountain'.

POFADDER – This tiny remote Northern Cape town is the epitome of 'the middle of nowhere' and South Africa's version of Timbuktu. Whilst most think this town is named after the Afrikaans name for the puff adder snake, it is most likely named after the Khoisan captain, Klaas Pofadder.

WELCOME TO   WELKOM IN

POFADDER

R31 Hotazel 10

← Tweebuffelsmeteenskoot-morsdoodgeskietfontein

NICKNAMES

CAPE TOWN – The Mother City

PORT ELIZABETH – The Friendly City

JOHANNESBURG – Egoli (The City of Gold)

EAST LONDON – The Buffalo City

DURBAN - Ethekwini (The Bay)

PRETORIA- Jacaranda City

PIETERMARITZBURG – Sleepy Hollow

SOUTH AFRICA - Mzansi

STRANGE NAMES

BAARDSKEERDERSBOS - This Western Cape hamlet means 'Beard Shaver's Bush' because of a mythical spider that shaves its own hair off to build its nest.

BANGHOEK - This Western Cape town means 'Scared Corner' and is rumoured to get its title from the lions that lurked there.

TIETIESBAAI - It doesn't take much imagination to conclude that this bay got its name from either the smooth, round boulders dotted around the beach or the small rounded hill that looks onto the town that resembles a breast with a nipple. It is neither. The town is named after Pieter Pieterse.

KNAPDAAR - Literally meaning, 'Almost There,' this place doesn't have much besides a railway and a hill. So it can be said that its name stems from the momentum needed by the train to get up the hill.

BELA-BELA - Previously known as Warmbaths, this Sesotho word simply means 'Bubble Bubble', in reference to the hot water springs in this area.

SO THE STORY GOES...

COFFEE BAY - The story goes that in 1973 a ship transporting coffee beans met its untimely end resulting in coffee beans drifting ashore.

KAROO - Khoikhoi for 'Dry' and 'Land of Thirst', this area is known for its harsh, dry conditions.

MAMELODI - This was the name by which President Paul Kruger was known and means 'The Man who can Imitate Birds'.

LYDENBURG - The name means 'Town of Suffering,' due to the severity of the malaria in the region.

CAPE AGULHAS - The southern-most tip of Africa means 'The Gulf of Needles' and came to be because the coastline rocks, which are as sharp as needles, were treacherous for early explorers in their boats.

ROBBEN ISLAND - The iconic island got its name from the Dutch word for seals, 'robbe', seeing as the entire island is surrounded by them.

CLARENS - Named after the Swiss village to which Paul Kruger fled when Pretoria was invaded by the British. He died there whilst in exile.

HOTAZEL - This town in the Northern Cape is well… 'as hot as hell'.

NOBODY is a bustling area adjacent to the University of Limpopo. Some claim that a local landowner, when removed from his farm, said that 'Nobody' would live on the land. Others say that a body was left on the roadside awaiting a hearse to collect it for burial. When the hearse arrived, the body had mysteriously disappeared – leaving 'NO BODY'.

DIE HEL - Translated to mean 'The Hell', this small valley and community remained almost completely isolated and unknown until 1963 when an access road was finally carved down a mountain pass to the town. Now named Gamkaskloof, the origin of this name is unclear but it's not too difficult to understand why this part of the world is called 'Die Hel'.

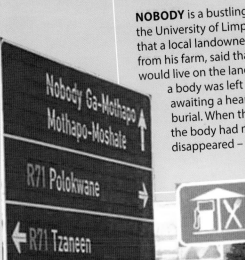

Freedom Day

From the earliest colonial times, South Africa's people were subject to White minority rule. For a period, Coloured and Black people in the Cape alone had limited voting rights, but over the years even these were taken away.

The 27th of April was the day in 1994 when the first democratic election was held in South Africa — all adults, irrespective of their race, could cast their ballot over a period of four days. On this same day in 1997, the new constitution came into effect. This document enshrined many human rights. After the first election, exiles returned from abroad and Nelson Mandela became South Africa's first democratically elected president. The 27th of April is now used by people to celebrate the end of apartheid and the beginning of democracy in South Africa, and to recommit to ensuring voting and living equality for all.

DEMOCRACY

HOPE

"
The truth is that we are not yet free; we have merely achieved the freedom to be free, the right not to be oppressed. We have not taken the final step of our journey, but the first step on a longer and even more difficult road; for to be free is not merely to cast off one's chains, but to live in a way that respects and enhances the freedom of others. The true test of our devotion to freedom is just beginning.
"

- Nelson Mandela

WARNING!

Africa is not for sissies!

KEEP A SAFE DISTANCE FROM ELEPHANTS

photos courtesy Facebook, Africa this is why I live here

Photo courtesy www.wildcard.co.za, Marlene Swart

Famous worldwide for its a cappella singing style, Ladysmith Black Mambazo is South Africa's best example of Isicathamiya or Mbube music. Rooted in Zulu culture, Isicathamiya is also strongly influenced by Western styles. The well-known hit *Graceland*, which Ladysmith Black Mambazo recorded with Paul Simon in 1986, is an excellent illustration. And of course, no-one will forget *Wimoweh* (also known as *The Lion Sleeps Tonight*) which was adapted from an Isicathamiya first hit song, Solomon Linda's *Mbube* (1939). Still enjoyed today, this powerful genre of popular South African music nevertheless dates back to the slum days of the 1800s when it reflected the experiences and struggles of generations of migrant workers. The music, typically performed in a cappella style by all-male groups singing various parts of harmony, still retains its original purpose of weekend entertainment for migrant workers and their families.

isicathamiya /mbube

mbaqanga

In the 1950s a fusion of Marabi, Kwela and American Jazz began emerging from the township of Sophiatown to form what would become a new Black urban music culture known as Mbaqanga. 'Mbaqanga' is Zulu for 'steamed maize bread'; quite a prophetic name for the genre considering how the music gathered steam in no time and took on a political stance as a tool to fight against apartheid laws. A whole new crop of musicians took to the stage and produced protest songs that got banned by the establishment. This included the music of some liberal Whites who joined their Black counterparts in the exciting night life of Sophiatown. Musicians to have popularised Mbaqanga include Miriam Makeba (with her iconic *Click Song*), Busi Mhlongo (notably for *Yehlisan' Umoya Ma-Afrika* [African Nation - calm]), Lucky Dube (before he switched to Reggae) and Johnny Clegg. Mahlathini (Simon Nkabinde) and the Mahotella Queens were a great commercial success in South Africa and surrounding countries. And the Soul Brothers - that slick outfit from KwaZulu-Natal - won international acclaim that culminated in a tour of the UK and Europe.

music genres

South African music is a rich and varied mix of old and new, foreign and local, political and peaceful. All genres from Isicathamiya to Kwaito and everything in between reflect the different people of SA, and have produced some of the most memorable songs and exciting musicians.

jazz

The brewing spot for Mbaqanga, Sophiatown was also the place for jazz in the 1950s. By around 1955 jazz had built a considerable following which resulted in the formation of the Sophiatown Jazz Club. The club mostly played the innovative music of artists like Charlie Parker and Dizzy Gillespie. Aspiring musicians would attend gatherings sponsored by the club. It was here that musicians like Dollar Brand (later Abdullah Ibrahim), Kippie Moeketsi, Jonas Gwangwa and Hugh Masekela, came together to form the Jazz Epistles, a bebop band that would shape the future of South African jazz. Since then the South African jazz scene has boomed both in stature and volume. In 1987 Hugh Masekela's hit single *Bring Him Back Home* became an anthem for the movement to free Nelson Mandela. And in 1988 Abdullah Ibrahim composed the award-winning soundtrack for Claire Denis's film *Chocolat*. Jazz festivals are now held throughout the country with the most popular being the Cape Town International Jazz Festival which is a two-day affair, featuring over 40 international and local bands that perform on multiple stages.

Rock and Pop

In the 1960s Rock and Pop groups, mainly aimed at White audiences, stirred things up in the country. *Master Jack* by Four Jacks and a Jill (one of SA's top pop group of the '70s) was a local hit that topped the charts in Europe and America. The '80s really saw things rolling with Afro-jazz bands like Bayete and Sakhile, a new genre called Bugglegum (popularised by Yvonne Chaka Chaka), and Brenda Fassie's legendary Township Pop. Fassie's best-known song, *Weekend Special*, together with her varied song collection, earned her the title *Queen of African Pop*. While the Black side of town really ticked, a White alternative rock culture began to develop with groups like The Cherry Faced Lurchers (who represented youthful rebellion against inhibitive segregation laws) and The Radio Rats whose satire mocked apartheid. A harder, guitar-driven rock emerged in the '90s, introduced by one of SA's finest rock bands, the Springbok Nude Girls. By this time Black and White musicians had started working together. The Afropop band, Mango Groove, as well as Johnny Clegg and Sipho Mchunu's famous *Juluka collaboration* is a great example of the fusion of traditional African music with White pop and rock.

Kwaito

With the dawn of democracy in 1994 came Kwaito – a South Africanised hip hop genre that became popular amongst post-apartheid Black youth. Kwaito is inspired by Chicago house musicians like The Fingers, Tony Humphries and Robert Owen, with synthesizers and other electronic instruments adding to the mix. Alongside Kwaito is a streetwise dance style that sees plenty of fierce dance battles in many parts of the country. Popular Kwaito musicians abound but some of the big names in the industry include Mdu, Mandoza (with his big crossover hit *Nkalakatha*), Arthur Mafokate (the King of Kwaito - check out one of his top songs *Vuvuzela*), Chiskop and Zola. Famous groups are Bongo Maffin, Abashante, Trompies, Boom Shaka and TKZee. These groups released chart-busting Kwaito hits that left their fans hollering for more - and more is what they are getting. For some youth, Kwaito has become a way of life, a way of being, with even a fashion style of its own. Like other genres, Kwaito has provided many talented youth with an opportunity to earn a decent living using their skills. No doubt Kwaito will be around for a long time to come.

Reggae

As well as rock and pop, Johnny Clegg is also known for popularising reggae during the 1980s. Together with other artists like O'Yaba, Clegg turned out reggae songs with political messages. In fact it was in the '70s that the music of such reggae greats as Peter Tosh and Burning Spear had started inspiring many South Africans in the fight against apartheid. *Gimme Hope Jo'anna*, by Eddy Grant, is a well-known anti-apartheid reggae anthem that was banned by the SA government when it was released in the '80s. But on the local scene it was James Mange and Lucky Dube who came to the fore. Mange, a Rastafari and reggae artist, was also a leading anti-apartheid activist who was imprisoned on Robben Island alongside Nelson Mandela and Walter Sisulu. And when Dube switched from Mbaqanga, he became the most successful reggae artist. His album *Slave* made him one of the best-selling artists in South African history. Reggae has continued to develop in South Africa transforming to Ragga and other forms. A thriving dancehall culture exists and Reggae continues to spread its message of peace, love and harmony.

Afrikaans

Back in the Great Trek days religious songs and the violin were typical Afrikaner music sounds. The concertina was then used to help develop the genre into what is famously known as 'Boeremusiek' (farmers' music). After 1905 Afrikaans composers came to the fore with the Afrikaans art song when poems were set to music, and at the end of World War II, they entered the opera scene with Mimi Coertse and others. But it is in the popular music field that Afrikaans music really made it big. This began in the late 1970s when the Musiek en Liriek (M en L - Music and Lyrics) genre re-energised the Afrikaans music scene. M en L's luisterliedjies (listen songs) contained 'loaded meanings' and several were banned by the government. The powers that were decried the music's morally corrupting influence and its foreign feel. But in the 1980s, musicians protested against the government's apartheid policy and its patriarchal nature and formed the industry-rocking Voëlvry Movement. Since the 1990s popular Afrikaans music has soared. Brassie vannie Kaap was the first group to rap in slang Afrikaans with their 2000 song *Potjiekos*. It inspired future zef-culture rappers Die Antwoord and Jack Parow.

THE WAR OF INDEPENDENCE

YEARS OF THE ANGLO-BOER WAR

How it all began

Out of defiance towards British rule in the Cape Colony, the Voortrekkers (Boers) moved inland between 1835 and 1845. This was in a desperate attempt to retain their independence and it resulted in the eventual formation of two inland Boer republics - the Orange Free State and the Transvaal. These republics quickly developed into an established nation with their own customs, rules, language and systems of government. In 1886 the Boers, under the rule of Paul Kruger, found gold, more gold than had ever been found in the world until then. Kruger saw a serious threat to Afrikaner independence develop as huge numbers of newcomers, mostly British, descended upon the gold fields. These newcomers were referred to as *uitlanders* (outlanders) by the Boers. The *uitlanders* began to grow restless under the laws of the Boers and they pushed for a right to vote in the Transvaal elections. Kruger realised that without urgent action, the *uitlanders* would soon qualify for the vote. His response was to implement a 14-year residence stipulation which spurred growing discontent amongst the *uitlanders*.

How it all ended

The *uitlanders* turned to the powerful British monarch for help. But unsuccessful negotiations between the British and Boer authorities resulted in a war. Up to half a million British soldiers squared up against some 65 000 Boers; Black South Africans were pulled into the conflict on both sides. Britain's military reputation suffered a blow as the Boers laid siege to Ladysmith, Kimberley and Mafeking. With time, the British offensive gained force, and by 1900 Bloemfontein, Johannesburg and Pretoria were occupied and Kruger fled for Europe. The Boer reply was to intensify guerilla warfare and in response the British adopted a scorched-earth policy and set up civilian concentration camps in which some 26 000 Boer women and children and 14 000 Black and Coloured people were to die in appalling conditions.

The war ended in Boer defeat with the Peace of Vereeniging in 1902. The Boers opted for peace on the basis of British suzerainty, with promises of local self-government, the swift restoration and efficient management of the gold mines, and, crucially, the alliance of Boers and Britons against Black Africans. The aftermath of the war, however, saw a long-lasting contention between English-speaking and Afrikaans-speaking South Africans.

Ten facts about the War

1 No more than 88 000 Boer men fought the strength of nearly 500 000 British Troops.

2 Australia, Canada and New Zealand sent troops to help the British. Irish volunteers sided with the Boers.

3 The Guinness Book of Records lists the Anglo-Boer War as Britain's most costly war outside of the two World Wars.

4 Over 360 000 horses were shipped to South Africa for the war. The Horse Memorial in Port Elizabeth is in honour of the 300 000 horses that were killed during the war.

5 Winston Churchill, who was a young war correspondent, after being captured made a daring escape from a military prison in Pretoria.

6 During the war Paul Kruger fled to Switzerland where he died in exile.

7 It was the first time in the world that camouflage was ever used. The Boers used it to blend into the treeless landscapes.

8 The world's first news footage and propaganda films were used during the war.

9 The Kop end in Liverpool's football stadium is named in honour of the British soldiers who fought in the battle of Spioenkop.

10 A memorial expressing their sympathy for President Kruger and his cause was signed by 29 000 American schoolboys (girls were excluded). A schoolboy was selected to travel to Pretoria to personally present the signatures to Kruger. The signatures were handed over together with a collection of newspaper clippings and pictures about the war in a large book packaged in a leather case.

IF
by Rudyard Kipling

If you can keep your head when all about you
Are losing theirs and blaming it on you,
If you can trust yourself when all men doubt you,
But make allowance for their doubting too;
If you can wait and not be tired by waiting,
Or being lied about, don't deal in lies,
Or being hated, don't give way to hating,
And yet don't look too good, nor talk too wise:

If you can dream - and not make dreams your master;
If you can think - and not make thoughts your aim;
If you can meet with Triumph and Disaster
And treat those two impostors just the same;
If you can bear to hear the truth you've spoken
Twisted by knaves to make a trap for fools,
Or watch the things you gave your life to, broken,
And stoop and build 'em up with worn-out tools:

If you can make one heap of all your winnings
And risk it on one turn of pitch-and-toss,
And lose, and start again at your beginnings
And never breathe a word about your loss;
If you can force your heart and nerve and sinew
To serve your turn long after they are gone,
And so hold on when there is nothing in you
Except the Will which says to them: 'Hold on!'

If you can talk with crowds and keep your virtue,
Or walk with Kings - nor lose the common touch,
If neither foes nor loving friends can hurt you,
If all men count with you, but none too much;
If you can fill the unforgiving minute
With sixty seconds' worth of distance run,
Yours is the Earth and everything that's in it,
And - which is more - you'll be a Man, my son!

Inspiring for over a century

The poem 'If', which was written by Rudyard Kipling, was inspired by Dr Leander Starr Jameson. In 1895 Jameson led a raid by British forces against the Boers in South Africa. The defeat increased the tensions that ultimately led to the Second Boer war.

Two of its most resonant lines, 'If you can meet with Triumph and Disaster and treat those two imposters just the same', stand above the players' entrance to the Centre Court at Wimbledon.

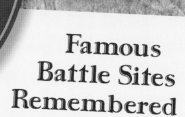

Famous Battle Sites Remembered

Majuba Hill: The first Anglo-Boer War ended in 1881 with a Boer victory at the Battle of Majuba Hill.

The Siege of Kimberley: A number of battles were fought in the Kimberley area, while the town itself was held under siege for 124 days.

The Siege of Ladysmith: Ladysmith is a gateway to a number of battle sites, not least the Battle of Spioenkop, where the British were defeated in their attempt to relieve the protracted siege.

Talana Museum, Dundee, KwaZulu-Natal: This excellent museum covers not only the Anglo-Boer Wars, but also the Anglo-Zulu Wars of the area.

National Women's Memorial and Anglo-Boer War Museum, Bloemfontein, Free State: This memorial commemorates the 26 000 Boer women and children who died in the British concentration camps during the second South African War.

Mafikeng, North West: Another town under siege in the South African War, Mahikeng (previously known as Mafikeng) has a number of magnificent tales to tell.

The Battlefields Route: The Battlefields Route in the Free State province takes history buffs on a journey through the areas where fierce fighting waged between the British and Boers at the start of the 20th century.

OUR ANTHEM

While *Die Stem* was being sung as the anthem of an apartheid government, *Nkosi Sikele' iAfrika* gained its popularity as a struggle song. In 1994 *Die Stem van Suid Afrika (The Call of South Africa)* and *Nkosi Sikelel' iAfrika (God bless Africa)* were combined and proclaimed as the official South African anthem.

NKOSI SIKELEL' IAFRIKA ⇨ GOD BLESS AFRICA
(English Translation)

Nkosi Sikele' iAfrika is a hymn, a prayer that calls for God's blessing on the land and its people. The first two stanzas were written and composed by Enoch Sontonga in 1897. Sontonga was a distinguished poet and school choirmaster. The amaXhosa poet, Samuel Mqhayi, wrote seven additional stanzas for the hymn and by 1925 it had become the official song of the African National Congress. Nokutela Dube, a musician, and her husband John Langalibalele Dube, worked tirelessly as fundraisers and promoters of African education. Part of their effort led to the popularisation of *Nkosi Sikele' iAfrika*.

Lord, bless Africa;
May her horn rise high up;
Hear Thou our prayers And bless us.

Chorus
Descend, O Spirit,
Descend, O Holy Spirit.

Bless our chiefs, May they remember their Creator.
Fear Him and revere Him,
That He may bless them.

Bless the public men, Bless also the youth
That they may carry the land with patience
and that Thou mayst bless them.

Bless the wives, And also all young women;
Lift up all the young girls
And bless them.

Bless the ministers of all the churches of this land;
Endue them with Thy Spirit
And bless them.

Bless agriculture and stock raising
Banish all famine and diseases;
Fill the land with good health
And bless it.

Bless our efforts of union and self-uplift,
Of education and mutual understanding
And bless them.

Lord, bless Africa. Blot out all its wickedness
And its transgressions and sins,
And bless it.

DIE STEM ⇨ THE CALL OF SOUTH AFRICA
(English translation)

Die Stem van Suid Afrika, part of which is included in the current anthem, was the only official anthem of South Africa from 1957 to 1994. It is a poem written by C.J. Langenhoven in May 1918. The music was composed by the Reverend Marthinus Lourens de Villiers in 1921. A recitation of *Die Stem* by Afrikaans actress, Hermione Faure, made a great contribution to its acceptance.

Ringing out from our blue heavens,
from our deep seas breaking round;
Over everlasting mountains
where the echoing crags resound;
From our plains where creaking wagons
cut their trails into the earth
Calls the spirit of our Country,
of the land that gave us birth.
At thy call we shall not falter,
firm and steadfast we shall stand,
At thy will to live or perish,
O South Africa, dear land.

In our body and our spirit, in our inmost heart held fast;
In the promise of our future and the glory of our past;
In our will, our work, our striving,
from the cradle to the grave
There's no land that shares our loving,
and no bond that can enslave.
Thou hast borne us and we know thee.
May our deeds to all proclaim
Our enduring love and service
to thy honour and thy name.

In the golden warmth of summer, in the chill of winter's air,
In the surging life of springtime, in the autumn of despair;
When the wedding bells are chiming
or when those we love depart,
Thou dost know us for thy children
and dost take us to thy heart.
Loudly peals the answering chorus:
We are thine, and we shall stand,
Be it life or death, to answer to thy call,
beloved land.

In Thy power, Almighty, trusting,
did our fathers build of old;
Strengthen then, O Lord, their children
to defend, to love, to hold -
That the heritage they gave us
for our children yet may be:
Bondsmen only to the Highest
and before the whole world free.
As our fathers trusted humbly,
teach us, Lord, to trust Thee still :
Guard our land and guide our people in
Thy way to do Thy will.

THEN AND NOW...

South Africa's national anthem, known as *Nkosi Sikelel' iAfrika*, was born out of conflict but today celebrates peace and unity in diversity. It expresses gratitude for the blessing of its people and unites South Africans of all professions and religions.

THE OFFICIAL NATIONAL ANTHEM

Nkosi sikelel' iAfrika
Maluphakanyisw' uphondo lwayo,
Yizwa imithandazo yethu,
Nkosi sikelela, thina lusapho lwayo.

Morena boloka setjhaba sa heso,
O fedise dintwa le matshwenyeho,
O se boloke, O se boloke setjhaba sa heso,
Setjhaba sa South Afrika - South Afrika.

Uit die blou van onse hemel,
Uit die diepte van ons see,
Oor ons ewige gebergtes,
Waar die kranse antwoord gee,

Sounds the call to come together,
And united we shall stand,
Let us live and strive for freedom,
In South Africa our land.

ENGLISH TRANSLATION

Lord, bless Africa
May her spirit rise high up
Hear thou our prayers
Lord bless us.

Lord, bless Africa
Banish wars and strife
Lord, bless our nation
Of South Africa.

Ringing out from our blue heavens
From our deep seas breaking round
Over everlasting mountains
Where the echoing crags resound.

Sounds the call to come together,
And united we shall stand,
Let us live and strive for freedom,
In South Africa our land.

Illustration courtesy of Cara Stirton

SOUTH AFRICA'S 11 OFFICIAL LANGUAGES

HOME LANGUAGES
Source: Census 2011

9.1%
Northern Sotho
4 618 576
speakers

7.6%
Sesotho
3 849 563
speakers

2.5%
siSwati
1 297 046
speakers

4.5%
Xitsonga
2 277 148
speakers

13.5%
Afrikaans
6 855 082
speakers

8%
Setswana
4 067 248
speakers

2.1%
isiNdebele
1 090 223
speakers

2.4%
Tshivenda
1 209 388
speakers

2.1%
Other
1 062 913
speakers

9.6%
English
4 892 623
speakers

16%
isiXhosa
8 154 258
speakers

22.7%
isiZulu
11 587 374
speakers

HOW TO SAY H•E•L•L•O

English: **Hello**

Afrikaans: **Goeiedag / Hallo**

isiNdebele: **Lotjhani**

Sesotho: **Dumela (singular) / Dumelang (plural)**

Northern Sotho: **Dumela (singular) / Dumelang (plural)**

Setswana: **Dumela (singular) / Dumelang (plural)**

siSwati: **Sawubona**

Xitsonga: **Avuxeni**

Tshivenda: **Ndaa (male) / Aa (female)**

isiXhosa: **Molo (singular) / Molweni (plural)**

isiZulu: **Sawubona (singular) / Sanibonani (plural)**

'IF YOU TALK TO A MAN IN A LANGUAGE HE UNDERSTANDS, THAT GOES TO HIS HEAD. IF YOU TALK TO HIM IN HIS LANGUAGE, THAT GOES TO HIS HEART'

– NELSON MANDELA

Afrikaans, the youngest language in the world

More Black, Coloured and Indian South Africans speak Afrikaans at home than White South Africans. Only 40 % of Afrikaans home speakers are White.

First known as Cape Dutch, it has its roots in 17th century Dutch, with influences from English, Malay, German, Portuguese, French and some African languages.

English and Afrikaans were declared official languages of the Union of South Africa in 1925.

The 1976 schoolchildren's uprising was due to the proposed imposition of Afrikaans in township schools.

The Xhosa Click

The second most common home language in South Africa involves three types of clicks – denoted by the letters C, X and Q. Xhosa is pronounced: '<Click!>osa'.

The 'C' click is made by placing the tip of the tongue on the roof of the mouth near the incisors and making a 'tsk tsk' sound.

For the 'X' click, you place the side of the tongue against the teeth and inhale, making a clicking sound.

The 'Q' click is produced by placing the tip of the tongue against the roof of the mouth and snapping it downwards. If you do it right, you should make a loud 'clop' sound.

80 % of learners

In the wider educational setting use English, followed by Afrikaans (16 %) and isiZulu (6 %).

Similarities

Many of South Africa's linguistic groups share common ancestry. As groupings and clans broke up in search of independence and greener pastures for their livestock, variations of the common languages evolved.

IsiZulu, isiXhosa, siSwati, and isiNdebele are collectively referred to as the Nguni languages, and have many similarities in syntax and grammar. The Sotho languages – Setswana, Northern Sotho, and Sesotho – also have much in common.

Fanagalo

A simplified version of isiZulu and isiXhosa which blends bits of English, Dutch, Afrikaans and Portuguese.

Fanagalo means 'do it like this'.

It was born on the mines during the colonial era so that White supervisors and African labourers could communicate.

Tsotsi Taal

An evolving language widely spoken in urban areas for communication between different language groups, it is a mix of Afrikaans, English and several indigenous languages with new words and phrases emerging regularly.

The word 'tsotsi' means 'gangster' or 'hoodlum' and 'taal' is Afrikaans for 'language'.

Did you know?
Over 230 000 South African people use Sign language as their home language.

Did you know?
English is the most understood language but only the fourth most spoken language.

An Ancient Civilisation

Sophisticated – Prosperous – Skilled

An Ancient Civilisation

One thousand years ago, the ancient city of Mapungubwe ('place of the jackal') was the centre of the largest kingdom in the African subcontinent. This Iron Age archaeological site in the Limpopo Province on the border between South Africa, Zimbabwe and Botswana, dates back to a city which existed from around 950 to 1300 AD.

The people cultivated a variety of crops such as millet, sorghum and possibly even cotton. They owned livestock and were well versed in the art of smelting iron, copper and gold, shaping the metal into both practical implements and decorative jewellery.

Highly Sophisticated

Archaeologists have found compelling evidence of this ancient, advanced civilisation with a significantly high culture and social hierarchy. Remnants of iron tools, clay pots, glass and gold artefacts can be found. An entire palace was discovered with burial sites of kings richly adorned in jewellery made from ivory, gold and copper, and porcelain and glass pearls.

Prosperous Traders

Due to their attraction to gold, as well as ivory, rhino horn and animal hides, Mapungubwe traded with Arabia and India (centuries before the Portuguese traders arrived). An extensive network formed through the East African ports via the Limpopo River which connected the region through trade to the ports of Kilwa and other sites along the Indian Ocean.

The golden rhino which was excavated in 1933, is made of gold foil nailed around a wooden interior which has delicately formed ears, horn and an upright tail.

1000 Years ago (900 - 1300 AD)

Illustration courtesy Johan Delanoire from the book
Mapungubwe by Tom Huffman. Wits University Press

Demise of the Capital

Mapungubwe's demise was brought about by climatic change. Cooler and drier conditions in the Limpopo/Shashe valley impacted on agriculture and by 1300 AD, the land could no longer sustain the high population. The inhabitants dispersed and Mapungubwe's position as a power base shifted north to Great Zimbabwe and later, Khami.

An Archaeological Treasure

Legends and rumours about the place were passed from generation to generation, but its secrets remained hidden for centuries. On New Year's Eve in 1932, a member of the community named Mowena took a local farmer, E.S.J. van Graan, to Mapungubwe Hill, where they found stone walls, iron and gold artefacts, pottery and beads. The find was soon reported to the History Department at the University of Pretoria. Within six months the government had purchased the site to prevent uncontrolled exploitation of its treasures and commissioned the university to undertake proper archaeological research.

Mapungubwe Cultural Landscape, Limpopo

lekker by die see!

(it's good at the beach!)

My chommies and I scored a jol at the larney's beach possie for

My friends and I had the opportunity of a fun time at the boss's beach house for

mahala. We were so amped 'cause we smaak that place, and people

free. We were so excited because we really like that place and people

pay big bucks to stay there. It's yonks since we went away. My sis packed

pay a lot of money to stay there. It's a long time since we went away. My sister packed

us some lekker sarmies nogal for padkos but, ag no man, my

us some delicious sandwiches as well for snacks on the road but, oh dear, my

boet is such a moegoe. He was so busy saying cheers to the toppies and

brother is such an idiot. He was so busy saying goodbye to our parents and

the laaitie that he forgot to pack the cooler box in the kombi. It made

younger brother that he forgot to pack the cooler box in the minivan. It made

me mal because we had to kak en betaal for chow. In the arvie

me cross because we had to pay a lot for food. In the afternoon

we put on our cozzies and slip slops one time and went to check

we put on our bathing suits and beach thongs straight away and went to look

out the surf. The guys went for a dip and the chicks decided to catch a

at the surf. The men went for a swim and the ladies decided to

tan. My boet was picking up stompies and he got dikbek when he

suntan. My brother was eavesdropping and got grumpy when he

heard us **tjooning** about how **dof** he was. He was **sommer** in a **dwaal**

heard us speaking about how stupid he was. He was just daydreaming

and **saw** his **gat** on the rocks. We got a **skrik** 'cause he hit his **pip** quite

and slipped on the rocks. We got a fright because he hit his head quite

bad. **shame**, it was **eina** but afterwards he was **hundreds**. **lish**, some

badly. Poor chap, it was sore but afterwards he was alright. Wow! Some

digs mates **rocked up** and we had a **dop** and some **chips** and **gooied** some

housemates arrived and we had a drink and some potato crisps and put some farm

wors and **sosaties** on the **braai**. **jislaaik!** I had a **babalas** and felt so

sausages and kebabs on the barbeque. Whew! I had a hangover and felt

swak in the morning. The other **okes** were still **dossing** so I went **on my**

terrible in the morning. The others were still sleeping so I went on my

ace for a jog. It was such a **schlep** to pack up

own for a jog. It was such a big job to pack up

and **waai** but I was so **stoked** 'cause

and leave but I was so pleased because

we had such a **lank jol**.

we had such a good time.

jo! We **checked** this **fundi** making sand art of a **vrecked** dude!

Oh my! We saw this expert making sand art of a skeleton!

LEADING - THE - WORLD

- GRAEME SMITH -

Graeme Smith is not only South Africa's youngest captain but also holds the world record for captaining the most Test matches, as well as for the highest number of wins in Tests as a captain. He also holds the world record for the most number of catches made in test matches by a non-wicketkeeper.

- HASHIM AMLA -

Hashim Amla, captain of the Test side, was chosen as South African Sports Star of the Year in 2011. He has held the title of The Best Batsman in the world in both Tests and ODIs as well as the record for the fastest player to reach both 5000 runs and 20 centuries in ODIs. He was chosen as one of Wisden's 2013 Cricketers of the Year.

- AB DE VILLIERS -

Abraham Benjamin de Villiers is captain of the national ODI side. De Villiers became the second-youngest and second-fastest South African to reach 1000 test runs after Graeme Pollock. He earned his rating as the world's top-ranked batsman when he became the record holder of the fastest 50, 100, and 150 in ODI history.

- JOHN SMIT -

John Smit captained the side which held up the 2007 Rugby World Cup trophy. At the time of his retirement, Smit was the most-capped Springbok and the most-capped international captain in the history of the game. He led the Boks in 83 of the 111 Tests in which he played. In 2011, he was inducted into the IRB Hall of Fame.

THE PROTEAS are the first team in history to be ranked simultaneously as the **top team** in Test matches, ODIs and T20s.

SPRINGBOK accolades include winning the World Cup, the Rugby Championship (previously the Tri Nations) and the Sevens World Series. They have been top of the **World Rugby Rankings** and were named 2008 **World Team of the Year** at the Laureus World Sports Awards.

The 2010 **FIFA WORLD CUP** was watched by 3.2 billion people in every country on Earth (almost half the world). Over 300 000 international tourists arrived for the World Cup with more than 95 % of them saying they would visit again, resulting in a radical change in attitudes by foreigners towards South Africa.

- GARY TEICHMANN -

With Teichmann as captain, the Springboks became regarded as the greatest Springbok team in history. His Springbok team won 27 of their 36 matches. Teichmann steered them through an undefeated Tri-Nations series and then to a world-record-equalling 17 consecutive Test wins, making him one of South Africa's most respected and successful captains.

- FRANCOIS PIENAAR -

When captain Francois Pienaar accepted the Rugby World Cup from Nelson Mandela in front of a home crowd in 1995, it made history around the world. Pienaar was voted International Player of the Year by *Rugby World* magazine. He is listed in both the International Rugby Hall of Fame and the IRB Hall of Fame.

- LUCAS RADEBE -

Lucas Radebe captained Bafana Bafana for the first-ever World Cup appearance in France. He also played for Leeds United during which time they won the Premier league on two occasions and was appointed their captain in 1998. Radebe was awarded the FIFA Fair Play award, which is rarely given to individuals. Nelson Mandela said of Lucas, 'This is my hero!'

- AARON MOKOENA -

Aaron Mokoena is the youngest-ever player to have represented South Africa. With over 100 caps he is also South Africa's most-capped soccer player. When he led Bafana Bafana as captain onto the field for the 2010 World Cup, they had a 12-match unbeaten record. Mokoena also played for Blackburn Rovers and Portsmouth.

BAFANA BAFANA hosted and won the 1996 **Africa Cup of Nations** and, in the process, reached 16th in the FIFA rankings. They followed this with a second-placed finish at the 1998 Africa Cup of Nations.

Bafana Bafana, which means **'THE BOYS'**, is South Africa's national football side. The support for 'The Boys' united South Africans in the lead-up to the 2010 **FIFA world cup** as the nation turned green when supporters of all ages around the country donned Bafana Bafana jerseys every Friday.

WORKERS' DAY

International Workers' Day is celebrated on 1 May around the world. It originated in the industrial struggle for an eight-hour day and now celebrates the working classes who developed the international labour movement.

South Africa's own Worker's Day adds further to this story. Due to the prohibitions placed on Black nationalist organisations during apartheid, Black workers took matters into their own hands in 1973 by organising strikes, which in turn led to the advancement of labour movements in the '80s. As the power of the trade unions grew, 1 May became unofficially known as Workers' Day. It wasn't until 1994 that Workers' Day was commemorated as an official public holiday - a recognition by the government of the efforts from the trade unions, Communist Party and labour groups who fought for freedom during apartheid.

Nowadays, employers and workers are governed by just labour practices which are aligned to the International Labour Organisation. The day is now celebrated not only to commemorate the achievements of the labour movements in the '70s but to continue to ensure fair labour practices for the working class.

> **'The harder you work, the luckier you get'**
> - Gary Player, South African Golfer and Sportsman of the century

Trade unions in South Africa

South Africa's trade union movement is the largest and most disciplined on the African continent. It has played an influential role in determining labour market and industrial relations policies in the country. It has succeeded in making employers appreciate the benefits of negotiating with employees through their representative unions. The fruits of these negotiations have included agreements on union recognition, wages, conditions of service, workplace restructuring and retrenchments.

The Constitution provides for the right to join trade unions, and for unions to collectively bargain and strike. The Labour Relations Act has given workers and their unions redress through mediation, conciliation and arbitration. Trade union representation is now an accepted facet of industrial practice. All workers have the right to join trade unions and they are legally protected against discrimination by employers for being union members.

The percentage of union membership has dropped from 45.2 % in 1997 to 25.04 % in 2012. This percentage would be **significantly** lower if it were not for government employees.

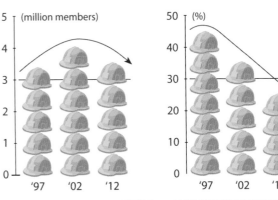

NO. OF TRADE UNION MEMBERS

% OF UNIONISATION OF WORKFORCE

Source: Africa Survey by the Institute of Race Relations

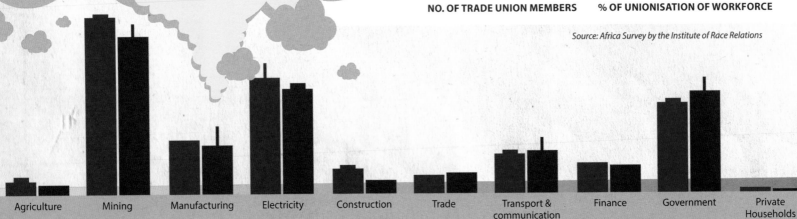

Agriculture | Mining | Manufacturing | Electricity | Construction | Trade | Transport & communication | Finance | Government | Private Households

Unionisation rate of industry sectors ■ 2000 ■ 2012

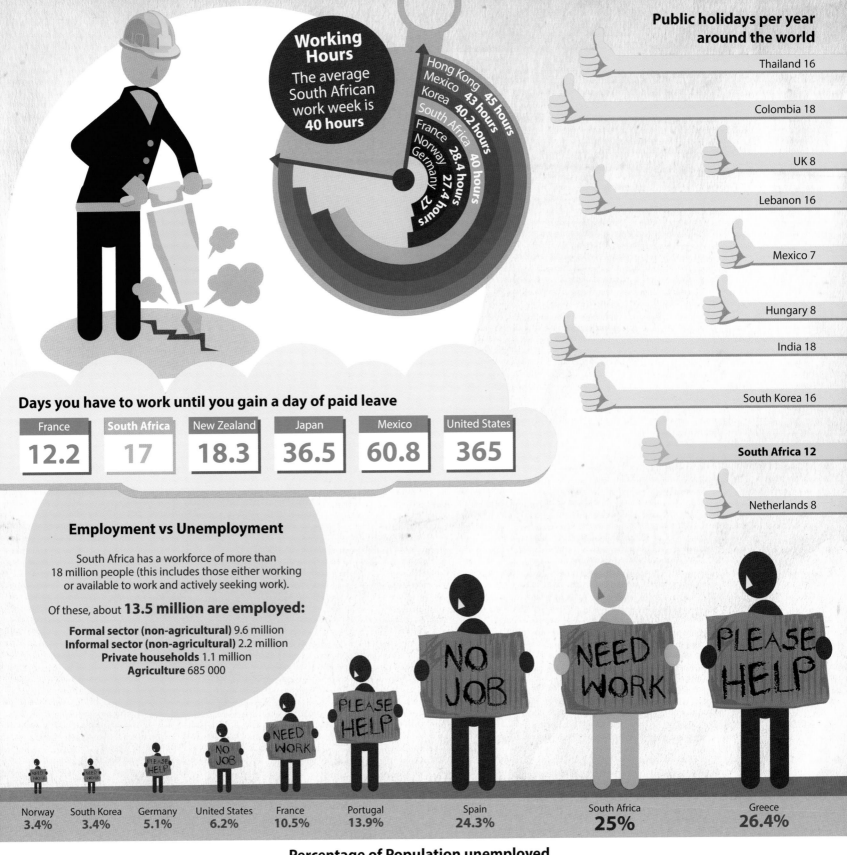

Working Hours
The average South African work week is **40 hours**

Hong Kong 45 hours
Mexico 43 hours
Korea 40.2 hours
South Africa 40 hours
France 28.4 hours
Norway 27.4 hours
Germany 27

Public holidays per year around the world

Thailand 16
Colombia 18
UK 8
Lebanon 16
Mexico 7
Hungary 8
India 18
South Korea 16
South Africa 12
Netherlands 8

Days you have to work until you gain a day of paid leave

France	South Africa	New Zealand	Japan	Mexico	United States
12.2	17	18.3	36.5	60.8	365

Employment vs Unemployment

South Africa has a workforce of more than 18 million people (this includes those either working or available to work and actively seeking work).

Of these, about **13.5 million are employed:**

Formal sector (non-agricultural) 9.6 million
Informal sector (non-agricultural) 2.2 million
Private households 1.1 million
Agriculture 685 000

Norway 3.4%
South Korea 3.4%
Germany 5.1%
United States 6.2%
France 10.5%
Portugal 13.9%
Spain 24.3%
South Africa **25%**
Greece 26.4%

Percentage of Population unemployed

THE KHOISAN PEOPLE

The San and Khoikhoi are descendants of the first people who lived in southern Africa, before Black or White people migrated into the region. The San were hunter-gatherers and ranged widely over the area. The Khoikhoi were pastoral and lived in the comparatively well-watered areas. The Khoikhoi used a word while dancing that sounded like 'Hottentots' and therefore settlers referred to the Khoikhoi by this name – however today this term is considered derogatory. The settlers used the term 'Bushmen' for the San, a term also considered derogatory today. Many of those whom the colonists called 'Bushmen' were in fact Khoikhoi or former Khoikhoi. For this reason, scholars sometimes find it convenient to refer to hunters and herders together as 'Khoisan'.

Geneticists say that the oldest gene pattern amongst modern humans is that of the Khoisan. It dates back to about 80 000 years ago. All other peoples on the planet, Europeans, Black Africans, Asians, North and South Americans, and Australians are all descendants of this original gene type.

The San are the best model that modern man has for the hunter-gatherer lifestyle that saw so many generations through the Stone Age. The 'toolkits' of the more modern San people are similar to artefacts found that date to the late Stone Age hunter-gatherers. Rock art by the late Stone Age hunter-gatherers can be found in the form of paintings or engravings in almost every district in South Africa.

Unfortunately, the Khoisan people have practically disappeared. That is, apart from the Nama, who are one of the last remaining Khoikhoi people living in Namaqualand, and the very small number of San people living mainly in Namibia and border areas of the Northern Cape Province.

The San are characterised by their very small stature, seldom over 1.5 m, and wrinkled appearance. They also have extremely keen eyesight. The San are skilled trackers and have an extraordinary flair for music and art.

The life of the San people was the focus of the film *The Gods Must Be Crazy* by Jamie Uys. When the movie was released in 1980 it was for a long time the highest-grossing foreign film ever released in the US.

Trouble stirrer
or Peace maker?

Albert Luthuli, Archbishop Emeritus Desmond Tutu, F.W. de Klerk and Nelson Mandela all won the Nobel Peace Prize and their effigies stand together at Cape Town's V&A Waterfront. Although not among the Nobel Laureates, the statues of legendaries Gandhi and Biko can be found in Pietermaritzburg and East London respectively.

Steve Biko

Stephen (Steve) Bantu Biko was the most prominent leader of the Black Consciousness Movement in South Africa and uncompromisingly stood out against the apartheid system of racial segregation. Although not a Nobel Laureate, Biko's actions and the government's reaction to them highlighted the cause of black people in SA and the country's suppression of freedom of speech. Biko was banned and detained several times by the apartheid authorities for his involvement in the liberation struggle and was arrested in 1977 and accused of writing inflammatory pamphlets and 'inciting unrest' among the Black community. His death in custody shortly thereafter drew the attention of the world to SA, sparking outrage.

'The most potent weapon in the hands of the oppressor is the mind of the oppressed.'
- Steve Biko, 1971.

Mahatma Gandhi

Mohandas Karamchand Gandhi was born in India, qualified as a lawyer in England, came to South Africa to work for an Indian law firm in 1893 and returned to India 21 years later. Whilst in South Africa, he boarded a first-class compartment train in Durban on 7 June 1893 but was evicted because he was Indian when the train reached Pietermaritzburg. Despite the treatment he received, Gandhi stayed on in SA for a further 21 years, tirelessly championing the rights of the oppressed and disenfranchised resident Indians. He formed the Natal Indian Congress in 1894 and was elected as the organisation's first secretary. This movement remained at the forefront of Indian political resistance for decades and eventually played a key role in the ANC's freedom struggle. In early 1900, Gandhi established a self-help settlement at Phoenix, Durban, which was devoted to his principles of passive resistance. It was here that he also founded the paper *Indian Opinion*, a newspaper that played an important role in spreading Gandhi's philosophy of passive resistance. Plinths, busts, statues and paintings in honour of this lauded troublemaker can be seen in various parts of KZN. A Salt March takes place every year to celebrate the lives of Gandhi and Chief Albert Luthuli, both of whom promoted Ubuntu and nonviolence.

'When Gandhi was evicted from the train, an Indian visiting South Africa fell, but when Gandhi rose, an Indian South African rose...Gandhi fell a passenger but rose a patriot, fell a barrister but rose a revolutionary... In fact, Gandhi was not flung here, he was launched.'
- Gopalkrishna Gandhi, Gandhi's grandson, 1997.

Chief Albert Luthuli

Albert John Mvumbi Luthuli (Chief Albert Luthuli) was South Africa's first Nobel Laureate and the first Black African to be awarded the Nobel Peace Prize (1960). In 1936, Luthuli was elected Chief of Groutville and in 1952, ANC president-general. When he participated in the Defiance Campaign of the same year, the apartheid government deposed him as chief and placed severe restrictions on his freedom. Despite banishment orders that lasted until his death in 1967, Luthuli led a campaign in 1962 together with Martin Luther King appealing for 'Action against Apartheid' from the United Nations. This troublemaker nevertheless advocated peaceful resistance to racial discrimination, appeared ambivalent about the ANC's armed struggle, and, as a Christian, famously said: 'The road to freedom is via the cross.'

Desmond Tutu

Archbishop Desmond Tutu was a central figure in the fight against apartheid and coined the phrase 'Rainbow Nation'. In 1984, he was awarded the Nobel Peace Prize for his untiring efforts in calling for an end to White minority rule in South Africa. Eleven years later, the new democratic government appointed him chair of the Truth and Reconciliation Commission. Despite these honours Tutu has riled many on both sides of the political spectrum, by, among other things, leading protest marches, speaking out against the homeland system and criticising the new government for not living up to its democratic ideals.

'I am not interested in picking up crumbs of compassion thrown from the table of someone who considers himself my master. I want the full menu of human rights.' - Desmond Tutu.

F.W. de Klerk

Less than a year after Frederick Willem de Klerk became President of SA in 1989, he announced that Nelson Mandela would be unconditionally released from prison. The announcement took many people by surprise and incurred opposition from political opponents and his own party alike. However, it helped quell the violence the country was experiencing and paved the way towards the end of apartheid. He was awarded the Nobel Peace Prize in 1993 for helping achieve a peaceful transformation from apartheid to democracy.

'The new era which is dawning… will lift us out of the silent grief of our past and into a future in which there will be opportunity and space for joy and beauty - for real and lasting peace.' - F.W. de Klerk.

Nelson Mandela

In 1964, Nelson Mandela was charged with sabotage, high treason and conspiracy to overthrow the government. He was sentenced to life imprisonment. Thirty years later, this famous troublemaker became SA's first democratically-elected President. He was awarded the joint Nobel Peace Prize with F.W. de Klerk for their efforts in achieving the peaceful transformation from an apartheid regime to democracy.

'I have fought against White domination, and I have fought against Black domination. I have cherished the ideal of a democratic and free society in which all persons live together in harmony and with equal opportunities… if needs be, it is an ideal for which I am prepared to die.' - Nelson Mandela.

BREAKING WORLD RECORDS

11 OFFICIAL LANGUAGES

South Africa holds the record for the country with the MOST OFFICIAL LANGUAGES

THE LARGEST PIZZA EVER MADE

had a diameter of 37.4 m and weighed 12 190 kg, Norwood, 1990

LARGEST BAREFOOT RACE

1143 runners participated in the Grace Aid event in Durban, 2014

THE SMALLEST LIVING ADULT OSTRICH

named Tom Thumb, is 127 cm tall, at the Cape Town Ostrich ranch, 2011 *The average male ostrich is usually 1.8 - 2.7 m tall*

MOST JUICE EXTRACTED

by treading grapes was 21.17 litres from 50 kg of grapes in two minutes at the Whoosh Festival

THE FARTHEST DISTANCE

by stand-up paddleboard in 12 hours on open water is 130.1 km between Kommetjie and Langebaan set in 2013

THE LONGEST KEBAB

measured 2047.47 m, Newcastle, 2008

THE LONGEST CONTINUOUS ARCHERY MARATHON

was set in 27 hours by a 15-year-old in Grahamstown in 2005

OLDEST BUNGY JUMPER AT AGE 96

He was unaware that he had broken a world record until after his jump at Bloukrans Bridge Bungy in 2010

MOST BALLET KICKS

1199 continuous grand battements alternating legs, Kimberley 2005, (Done with apparent ease keeping both knees straight)

MOST YACHTS TO FINISH INLAND RACE

was 389 yachts in Deneysville in the Free State, 2007

GREATEST DISTANCE FLOWN IN A TANDEM PARAGLIDER

(without landing) was 356.2 km from Vosburg to Krompoort Farm in 2006

THE LONGEST DISTANCE RIDING A MOTORCYCLE

in 24 hours is 3256.5 km on Phakisa Freeway, Welkom, 2014

110 SURFERS ON ONE WAVE

Set in 2009 in Muizenberg, 110 surfers got up on one wave riding simultaneously in an effort to raise awareness of climate change

Source: WWW.GUINNESSWORLDRECORDS.COM

HOW TO MAKE BILTONG!

Learning how to make biltong the South African way is an immensely gratifying process. Not only will you save money and win friends, you'll also experience the unmistakeable bubbling sensation of patriotism.

YOU WILL NEED:

2 kg lean silverside or sirloin steak

Coarse salt and ground black pepper

Coarse ground coriander

Vinegar (preferably apple-cider vinegar)

Optional spices (paprika or cloves).

Save the Earth — it's the only planet with biltong

STEP 1:

MEAT SELECTION

Remove excess fat
(leave just enough for flavour)

Cut 20 cm lengths of meat

Slice into 10 cm thick strips
with the grain

Remove any
sinew or gristle.

≥ DO ≡

Always use fresh meat

Sterilise all equipment and surfaces

Hang the meat thickest part on top

Keep covered to keep flies away

Avoid humidity.

≥ DON'T ≡

Don't leave on too much fat -
fatty meats are more likely to
spoil during the drying process

Don't let the meat touch
the sides of the box

Don't let the pieces of
meat touch each other.

EXPERIMENT AND BE ADVENTUROUS

The History of Biltong

The word BILTONG is derived from the words 'BIL' (BUTTOCK) or meat and 'TONG' or strip. So it is just a strip of meat.

BILTONG, as we know this delicacy today, is a rich inheritance from our pioneering South African forefathers, who sun-dried meat during their trek across the African subcontinent. The indigenous Khoikhoi preserved meat by slicing it, curing it with salt, and hanging it up to dry. After European settlers arrived in the early 17th century, they improved the curing process by using vinegar, saltpeter and spices including pepper, coriander and cloves. The abundance of wild game provided the Voortrekkers with needed supplies of meat for their migration from the Cape Colony.

Difference between Biltong and Beef Jerky

Biltong meat is much thicker.

The vinegar, spices and the drying process of biltong give it more texture and flavour than jerky. Unlike jerky, biltong is never smoked.

Step 2:
Meat Preparation

Sprinkle with salt and leave to stand

Brush meat with vinegar

Hold meat up to drain off excess vinegar

Sprinkle with ground pepper and ground coriander.

Step 3:
Drying

Hang biltong in your biltong maker

If you don't have a biltong maker then an isolated dry and warm environment with adequate ventilation will suffice

Leave for anything from 24 hours to 10 days.

Step 4:

Eat And Enjoy!

How to make a Biltong Box

Use a sealed box (wood or even cardboard can be used) with holes in the sides or a fan. Add a 60 W lightbulb on the inside towards the bottom and insert dowel sticks in the top from which to hang the meat.

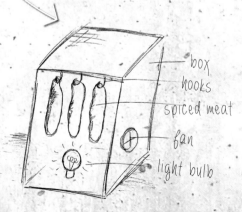

box
hooks
spiced meat
fan
light bulb

CULTURES & TRADITIONS

Photo © Steve Evans

Although westernisation and urbanisation are rapidly reducing tribal practices, more than half the people of South Africa are influenced by tribal values and customs.

LOBOLA

Lobola (or lobolo) is an age-old African custom whereby the groom gives a payment for a bride to her family as a token of appreciation for allowing him to marry their daughter. The payment is negotiated and traditionally is in the form of cattle. Modern families, however, might use cash payments. The lobola demonstrates respectability and how much the girl is valued by both sides. It is also aimed at bringing the two families together by developing mutual respect and showing that the groom is capable of financially supporting his future wife.

ANCESTOR WORSHIP

The spiritual life plays a significant role in the lives of both the Sotho and the Nguni groups, particularly the Zulu. Worship centres around the people's reverence for thier ancestors. According to tradition, when a person dies, he or she will continue to watch over his or her people from the spiritual world. Ancestors can, therefore, influence events on Earth. People honour their ancestors to receive protection and ward off evil spirits. The ancestors serve as intermediaries between the physical and the spirit world. They speak to the ancestors rather than to God directly, requesting God for help during difficult times. It is believed that all ancestors must be kept in the memory of the family otherwise, if forgotten, they may seek to be remembered by visiting trouble on them.

NDEBELE SPLENDOUR

The adornment and dress of the Ndebele women become increasingly spectacular after marriage and with age. It is customary for a Ndebele wife to wear copper or grass rings around her neck as well as around her arms and legs. Traditionally, the husband provides his wife with her rings and the more rings she wears the greater is her husband's wealth. The rings are considered by wives to be a token of bondedness and faithfulness to their husbands. The rings are believed to have strong ritual power and only, on the death of the husband, will they be removed.

Photo courtesy South African Tourism

FACE PAINTING

It is common to see groups, particularly amongst the Xhosa, with painted faces. A mixture of fat and red ochre, or soot, washing blue and white clay are used for facial decoration as well as for protection against the sun. The young male initiates cover their whole body with white clay during their initiation ceremony.

REED DANCE

The reed dance is an important rite of passage for young Zulu women. This is a colourful and cultural celebration that promotes respect for young women, and preserves the custom of keeping girls as virgins until marriage. Led by Zulu princesses, the young women form a sea of colour in intricately beaded outfits as they each collect a reed and present it to the king. While they are delivering the reed sticks, Zulu men also participate in this part of the ceremony, mock fighting and also singing and dancing. At this stage, the maidens are taught by senior females how to behave themselves and be proud of their virginity and naked bodies. This allows maidens to expect respect from the suitors who intend approaching them during the ceremony. The older sisters educate the young maidens on how to behave in married life. Young maidens are encouraged not to argue or respond immediately but to wish the suitor well on his journey back. In Zulu mythology, if a young woman who is not a virgin takes part in the reed-dance ceremony, her reed will break. The reed dance portrays and instils a sense of pride, belonging and identity among the youth.

Photo © MediaClubSouthAfrica, Rodger Bosch

KHWETHA CEREMONY

The initiation ceremony known as the *Ukwaluka* (circumcision) or the A*bakhwetha* ritual is the most important event in any male's life. This southern African ceremony is practiced by several tribes and is how a young boy proves his manhood. When they are of age, usually in their late teens, the boys are sent to spend several days or weeks in a circumcision lodge during winter. The boys are put through rigorous and often dangerous tests and rituals such as continuous dancing until exhaustion, and circumcision. The initiates are painted white with chalk or clay from head to foot and wrapped in blankets. They are then lectured on being honourable men. This event is seen as a rite of passage, particularly for the Xhosa. For medical reasons, the circumcision ceremony is becoming increasingly controversial.

LOVE LETTERS

Love letters are small, postage-stamp-sized plaques of beads given by Zulu maidens to convey an emotion to the recipient - usually a favourable or unfavourable inclination towards his advances. Prior to the introduction of glass beads, the Zulu girls would use seeds, ostrich eggshell and seashells for adornment. The colours of the beads bear different meanings.

THE MEANING OF THE LOVE LETTERS DEPENDS ON BOTH THE INDIVIDUAL AND COMBINATION OF COLOURS:

Black - Marriage/separation
Blue - Trust/hatred
Yellow - Luck/misadventure
Green - Happiness/sorrow
Pink - Powerful/lowly
Red - Love/heartache
White - Purity

They've got it Covered

South African Women stunning the world.

Believe in women power!

¹ Candice Swanepoel

This Mooi River model had the privilege of opening the first Victoria's Secret retail store in Canada and in 2013 claimed the coveted cover model title of the Victoria's Secret Swim Catalogue. She has received several accolades including being placed 10th on the Forbes top-earning models list; listed in *FHM's* annual '100 Sexiest Women in the World' poll; and voted number one on Maxim's 'Hot 100' list.

² Rolene Strauss

Studying medicine at the University of the Free State is not the only thing that's impressive about this brunette beauty with brains. She also holds the title, not only of Miss South Africa 2014, but of Miss World 2014. She was the third South African woman to hold the Miss World title, the second to win it outright, and the first South African crowned Miss World in 40 years.

³ Bonang Matheba

Bonang is a presenter on *Top Billing*, a radio presenter on Metro FM and a television host on *Mzansi Magic*. But that's not all there is to Bonang Matheba. She's: been a cover girl for magazines like *FHM* and *Elle*; won a number of prestigious awards; and launched a clothing range, a handbag range and lingerie range. On top of all this, she also finds time to be a Global Brand Ambassador for Revlon Cosmetics.

⁴ Charlize Theron

This South African beauty is now an award-winning actress in Hollywood. She is the first South African to win an Oscar for Best Actress. In 2005 she received a star on the Hollywood Walk of Fame and, in 2006, was listed as one of the highest-paid actresses in Hollywood. Theron has her own production company and also started The Charlize Theron Africa Outreach Project (CTAOP). She is actively involved in women's rights organisations and, in 2008, was recognised as a United Nations Messenger of Peace.

⁵ Phuti Malabie

'As a businesswoman my feminine side isn't a weakness, it's an absolute strength.'

Phuti, who has held the position as CEO of the Shanduka Group, was listed in the Wall Street Journal as one of the 'Top 50 women in the world to watch in 2008' and was recognised by Forbes Woman Africa as 'Businesswoman of the Year' in 2012.

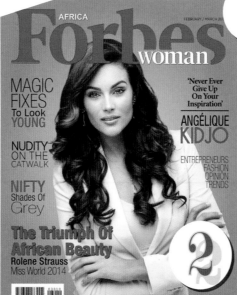

[6] Charlene
Wittstock

Charlene first became famous for representing South Africa as an Olympic swimmer. Her participation and success at the Olympics has led to her being named a Global Ambassador for the Special Olympics. However, the former swimming champion is now best known as the Princess of Monaco. This has seen her becoming involved in numerous humanitarian organisations, becoming an associate of the Nelson Mandela Foundation and being named co-patron of the Giving Organisation Trust - a group of South African Charities.

[7] Basetsana
Kumalo

Some may remember her being crowned Miss South Africa in 1994 but nowadays you may know her as a television personality on *Top Billing*. Basetsana also started the accredited production company, Tswelopele Productions, and held the title of President of the Businesswomen's Association of South Africa. She was voted 74th on the list of '100 Greatest South Africans' in 2004; was the face of Revlon Realistic Hair Care Range and a Revlon spokesperson; contributed to the book *Inspirational Women at Work*; and is the editor-at-large of the *Top Billing Magazine*.

[8] Lira

This multi-platinum selling and eight-times South African music award-winning vocalist has really made her mark in the South Africa music industry. She has also performed at the 2010 FIFA World Cup Kick-off Concert alongside international artists, been a cover girl for over 30 magazines worldwide, claimed awards from grassroots organisations, outreach groups, and advocacy programmes, made her cinematic debut as the support lead role in the Italian feature film *Consul* and has been an ambassador for major brands.

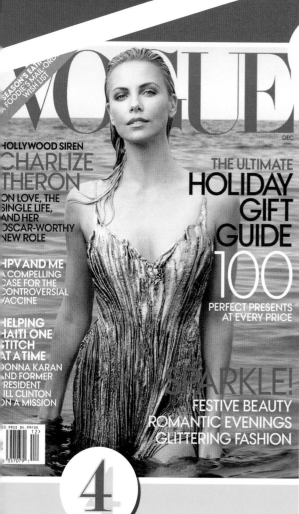

The oldest and largest

An explosion more than seven times greater than the Hiroshima Nuclear Bomb!

The growth and wealth of South Africa today is a result of this event which occurred over 2000 million years ago. The impact of the meteor was so great that it created a crater over 250 km wide and tens of kilometers deep. The force turned the Earth inside out, forcing gold-rich layers of rock to the surface. These gold deposits were protected with debris and fallen rock for millions of centuries. The rim of the crater forms the arc on which South Africa's gold mines lie. The outer circle of the impact forms what is known today as the Witwatersrand and stretches from either side of Johannesburg, through the West Rand and Klerksdorp to Welkom in the Free State.

Vredefort is the only example to provide a full geological profile of an astrobleme below the crater floor, allowing research into the genesis and development of an astrobleme immediately post-impact. The site contains high quality and accessible geological (outcrop) sites that demonstrate a range of geological evidences of a complex meteorite impact structure. The rural and natural landscapes of the area help to portray the magnitude of the ring structures resulting from the impact.

It's all north ... and sometimes no north... in the crater.

When you use a compass in the centre of the Vredefort crater, with each step forward the needle swings to a completely different quadrant. If you move the compass above the surface of a rock outcrop, with every few centimetres of motion the needle swings around. The probable source of Vredefort's weird magnetism was the strong and chaotic magnetic field produced at the height of the collision. In fact, scientists have calculated that a mere one-kilometre-wide asteroid, one tenth the size of Vredefort's, would create a field 1000 times that of the Earth at a distance of 100 km.

2023 million years ago

- an asteroid the size of Table Mountain crashed into Earth defining today's South Africa

meteor crater on earth

Despite the effects of erosion over the years the crater is still clearly visible from space

Vredefort Dome, Free State

SIGNS OF PROGRESS

I have learnt that a lot of things are wrong with South Africa: unemployment, inequality, and the lack of social capital.

But there are also an **enormous number of important things that are going right:** the corrective influences of an open society; the power of creative individuals; and the value of unlearning and learning anew.

- J.P. Landman, political-economic analyst

Number of individuals
GOING HUNGRY

Results from the General Household Survey show that self-reported hunger in South Africa has dropped from roughly 30 % in 2002 to just 13 % in 2011.

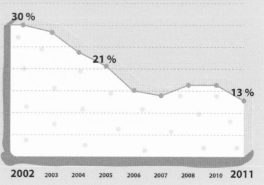

30 %

21 %

13 %

2002 2003 2004 2005 2006 2007 2008 2010 **2011**

Source: StatsSA, Poverty Trends in South Africa

SOUTH AFRICA RANKS
#1 IN THE WORLD
FOR ITS STRENGTH OF
AUDITING
AND REPORTING
STANDARDS

Source: Global Competitiveness Report 2014/15

ACCESS TO SANITATION

75.2 % of South Africans had access to sanitation in 1993, and by 2012 it increased to

81.7 %

compared to the world average of **79.3 %**.

Households with access to
ELECTRICITY

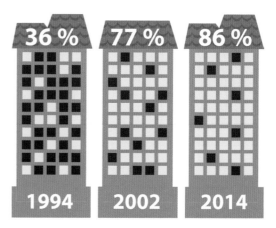

36 % — 1994

77 % — 2002

86 % — 2014

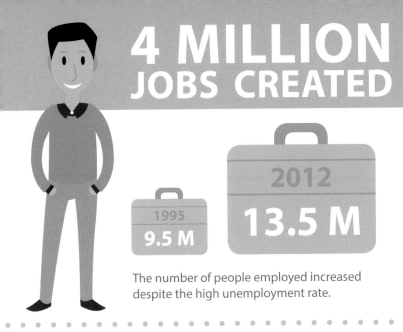

4 MILLION JOBS CREATED

2012
13.5 M

1995
9.5 M

The number of people employed increased despite the high unemployment rate.

EARNINGS

Average per person in real terms (without the distorting impact of inflation)

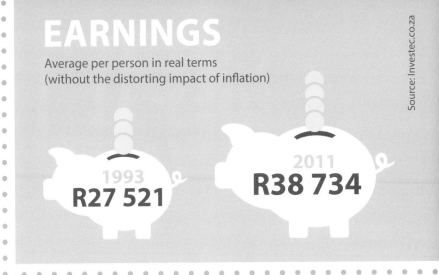

1993
R27 521

2011
R38 734

GROWTH IN THE MIDDLE CLASS

1993
3.6
MILLION PEOPLE

2012
7.2
MILLION PEOPLE

HOUSE PRICE INDEX

SOUTH AFRICA'S HOUSE PRICE IMPROVEMENT OVER FIVE YEARS IS RATED AMONGST THE

Source: The Economist

5 BEST COUNTRIES IN THE WORLD

ECONOMY GROWTH

Average GDP for the 16 years before 1993 **1.6 %**   Average GDP for the 16 years after 1993 **3.3 %**

| 1975 | The country got 11 % poorer over the 19 years between 1975 and 1993 | 1993 | 1994 | The country got 34 % richer over the 19 years between 1994 and 2012 | 2012 |

YOUTH DAY

'To really honour Youth Day, society needs to stop trying to define 'youth' as either a problem to deal with or an issue that can win elections. Young people need a voice in their own future.'

Photo © Nelle Laurens

The youth total 50 % of the entire population. The 15-24 year age group currently accounts for 20 % of the total population, some 10 million of them, whilst the 0-14 year age group forms 30 % of the population and number some 16 million.

Education in apartheid South Africa was a segregated affair which ensured that Blacks and Whites were schooled separately. Black schools had to conform to being taught half of the school curriculum in Afrikaans, the language of the ruling party - a decision which would spark an uprising.

The Soweto Students' Representative Council wanted to protest against this unfair policy as well as the terrible learning conditions of the schools. So, on 16 June 1976, a mass of students from Soweto and around the country rallied together to fight for a better education. What was supposed to be a simple protest turned tragic when police chose to open fire on the 20 000 learners, killing a number of them, including 12-year-old Hector Pieterson. This unexpected retaliation resulted in eight months of violent uprisings throughout South Africa, leaving in its wake 1000 dead and a number of people arrested. A protest which was initially about unfair education policies, evolved into a bigger conversation - an outcry against discrimination and human rights inequalities as a whole.

In 1994, at the first democratic elections, the new Constitution ruled in favour of prioritising children's rights, honouring the role that young people played in the establishment of democracy and the future of education in South Africa.

PATIENCE MTHUNZI

Dr Patience Mthunzi is a hybrid scientist. She has a Masters in biology, a PhD in physics, and an interest in various branches of science. She currently works in the biophotonics field, a new science involving the microscopic study of cells and molecules using laser light. Mthunzi is the first biophotonics PhD graduate in SA and the only one heading up this kind of research at the CSIR. She has received several awards including being named one of 20 'Youngest Power Women in Africa 2012' by Forbes Magazine.

NELISWA FENTE

Named by Youth Village as one of South Africa's Top 20 Inspiring Young People, Neliswa Fente's life truly reflects her passion for people, youth development and leadership. This 29-year-old has co-founded a youth organisation called SpringAGE, which is focused on encouraging youth to come up with innovative solutions for the future of the country. Neliswa is also an ambassador and board member for One Young World, was named a South African Spark Changemaker for 2013, and was selected to be a part of the World Economic Forum Global Shapers Community.

JONATHAN LIEBMANN

Jonathan Liebmann has shown that being just shy of 30 doesn't stop you from being the owner of one of the most thriving precincts in Johannesburg. In 2007 he founded Propertuity - a property development company - which was then used to launch the Maboneng Precinct among many urban development projects. Maboneng is all about re-purposing old industrial buildings and getting businesses and individuals on board to rejuvenate them. Jonathan's vision is to see cities transformed through the work that he does.

LUDWICK MARISHANE

Ludwick is a UCT commerce graduate who is most famous for inventing DryBath - a germicidal, waterless bath gel. This achievement is just one among many that this young man had accomplished by the time he graduated. Google named him one of the 12 'Brightest Minds in the World'; the Entrepreneurs' Organisation voted him Best Student Entrepreneur in the World in 2011 and he had made the finals of the Singapore University Global Business plan competition. He now owns his own company - Headboy Industries Inc. - through which he sells his patented invention.

NKOSI JOHNSON

Nkosi first came to public attention when a primary school refused to accept him because of his HIV-positive status. He made a powerful impact on public perception of the pandemic before his death at the age of 12 in 2001. He delivered a self-written speech at the 13th International AIDS Conference, during which he encouraged people with HIV/AIDS to be open about the disease and to seek equal treatment. The longest-surviving child born with HIV in the country at the time, he was ranked fifth amongst SABC3's 'Great South Africans' and Nelson Mandela referred to him as an 'icon of the struggle for life'.

VUSI THEMBEKWAYO

Motivational speaker, Vusi Thembekwayo, is a young businessman who has a lot to be proud of. Not only is he the owner of his own consulting business, Motiv8, but he is also an independent, non-executive director of RBA Holding - a property development group. This inspiring entrepreneur has received multiple awards and accolades - which isn't surprising given that he started a new business division at MetCash which he then converted into a R 461 million a year turnover business.

SIYABULELA XUZA

Siyabulela found his passion in utilising the power of the sun for clean, affordable energy. This passion turned into a science project that resulted in him developing a cheaper and safer form of rocket fuel. He had the opportunity of presenting his project to the King and Queen of Sweden in 2006 and he also attended the Nobel Prize Ceremony in Stockholm. His ingenious project then won two main awards at the Intel International Science & Engineering Fair in the USA. This achievement led to his travelling to various countries to speak about creating prosperity for Africa; and becoming the youngest member of the African Union-affiliated Africa 2.0 energy advisory panel.

RAPELANG RABANA

You know you're something special when you make Oprah's 2012 O-Power List. Rapelang Rabana *is the* founding CEO of Yeigo Communications - South Africa's first mobile VOiP company - and Global Head of Research and Development for the Swiss Telfree Group of Companies. She is also responsible for developing a mobile app called ReKindle Learning. The app is geared toward changing the way people transfer knowledge and approach education.

'WHENEVER I AM WITH ENERGETIC YOUNG PEOPLE, I FEEL LIKE A RECHARGED BATTERY.'
- NELSON MANDELA

Eating South African

...A TASTE EXPLOSION!

TRADITIONAL DELIGHTS

Morogo

Delectable wild spinach and pumpkin leaves, softened with butter-braised onions and tangy tomato. Served with Amadumbe mash (humble sweet potato).

Umngqusho

(It's as much of a mouthful as its name!)

A Xhosa delicacy of samp (maize kernels) mixed with boiled, seasoned beans.

Mogodu

Lightly curried tripe boiled with onions for two to three hours. Served with pap.

Shisa Nyama

Fresh from the butcher, your favourite meat flame-grilled to perfection in an outdoor kitchen, accompanied with secret traditional pap.

Shisa nyama is a Zulu phrase which literally means 'burn meat'.

ORDERS TO GO

Bunny Chow

For those that like it hot! A hollowed-out half loaf of fresh bread, filled with bean or mutton curry. This favourite dates back to when Blacks couldn't sit in restaurants. It was born when Durban Indian restaurant owners saw the need for a quick and convenient meal.

Gatsby

A Cape Town favourite, - a fully loaded roll stuffed with your choice of filling and compulsory slap chips (sloppy French fries).

It's messy, for sure, and just as delicious.

FARMHOUSE FAVOURITES

Tomato Bredie

An oldie, but a goodie! A Cape dish of succulent slow-stewed lamb and vegetables with cinnamon, cardamom, ginger, cloves and a hint of chilli. Served with steamed rice.

Venison Pie

Made with steaks of game, leisurely marinated until tender. Taste sensations include springbok, gemsbok and eland.

Frikkadels

Beef meatballs made with tomato, onion and fresh herbs. Served with mash and a thick gravy.

Bobotie

A trademark from the Cape Malays. Curried mince and baked egg topping, served with tangy fruit chutney on the side.

Sosaties

Skewers of marinated chicken, lamb or beef with seasonal vegetables flame-grilled on the braai. Served with pap and chakalaka.

Oxtail Potjie

The nation's meat and vegetable! Slow-cooked with fragrant cloves and red wine in a three-legged cast-iron pot over coals. Served with fresh roosterbrood.

SEAFOOD DELICACIES

Snoek
This tasty fish is caught off the Cape Coast and is smoked and braaied.

West Coast Seafood Platter
Delicious fresh mussels, crayfish, calamari and linefish caught by local fishermen. Linefish varieties include: yellowtail, hake, dorado and pole-caught tuna.

Perlemoen
Sourced fresh from legal abalone farms on the West Coast, some believe this shellfish is an aphrodisiac!

DID YOU KNOW
The Southern African Sustainable Seafood Initiative (SASSI) operates FishMS – an SMS service allowing consumers to receive feedback about sustainable choices. SMS the name of the fish to 079 499 8795.

SWEET TOOTH

Malva Pudding
A gift from the Dutch settlers, this one's best hot out the oven. Rich caramelised sponge with apricot jam, served with lashings of warm custard. Loosen your belts, it's comfort food personified!

Melktert - 'n Boer maak 'n plan, en 'n Boer maak 'n Melktert!
A buttery pastry shell, filled with a creamy milk custard and generously sprinkled with cinnamon. Order extra for tea tomorrow with Gogo (isiZulu for 'granny').

Koeksisters
Plaited twists of deep-fried dough, dipped in a sticky sweet syrup. Named after the hissing sound created by the Dutch dropping the dough into boiling oil.

Peppermint Crisp Fridge Tart
A modern-day favourite of real Bakers Tennis Biscuits, layered with Nestlé caramel treat and topped with cream and chunks of Peppermint Crisp chocolate.

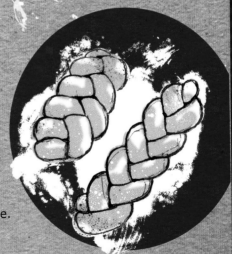

WANT TO BE A VEXILLOLOGIST?

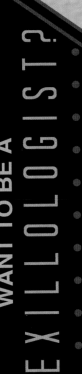

START HERE…
Vexillology is the study of flags. The word is a synthesis of the Latin word *vexillum* ('flag') and the Greek suffix *-logia* ('study').

THE SOUTH AFRICAN FLAG WAS FLOWN IN A DEMOCRATIC SOUTH AFRICA FOR THE FIRST TIME ON ELECTION DAY IN

1994

Originally commissioned as an interim flag it became such a powerful symbol of

UNITY + PATRIOTISM

that it has never been replaced

THE Y-SHAPED DESIGN

can be seen as the coming together, and the onward travel, of the different people of South Africa.

WHILST THE COLOURS HAVE

NO OFFICIAL SYMBOLISM

THEY DO REFLECT SOME OF OUR HISTORY

THE ONLY FLAG IN THE WORLD WITH

SIX COLOURS

Blue, white and red reflect the British and Dutch influence and formed part of the former South African flag

Green is thought to mean the unification of the various ETHNIC GROUPS

Black, green and gold feature in the flags of liberation movements such as the African National Congress and the Pan-Africanist Congress

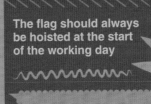

The flag should always be hoisted at the start of the working day and lowered again before or at sunset

THE FLAG SHOULD BE HOISTED BRISKLY AND LOWERED CEREMONIOUSLY

THE FLAG CANNOT BE USED TO COVER A STATUE OR PLAQUE AT UNVEILING OR SIMILAR CEREMONIES

The flag cannot be used to start or finish any competition, race or similar event

When the national flag is displayed **HORIZONTALLY** the hoist should be to the left of the spectator and the red band uppermost

When it is displayed **VERTICALLY** the red band should be to the left of the spectator with the hoist uppermost

In company with other national flags the national flag must always occupy the **POSITION OF HONOUR**

This means it must be the flag furthest to the right (observer's left) of all the flags on display with the flags of other countries being arranged alphabetically

Dotted lines represent pencil marks used as guides. These should be erased later. When you have finished, colour in the flag.

Whenever a person sees an official flag-hoisting or -lowering ceremony in progress he or she should come to a halt and stand respectfully to attention for the duration

THE SOUTH AFRICAN FLAG DOES NOT HAVE AN OFFICIAL NAME BUT SOME SUGGESTIONS INCLUDE:

THE WINDS OF **CHANGE**

FLUTTERING RAINBOW

Rainbow Warrior

Shosholoza

YEBO FLAG

Rainbow Pride

AmaFlappaFlappa

HOW TO DRAW THE FLAG

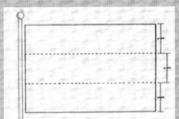

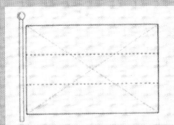

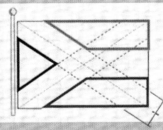

THE FLAG CANNOT BE USED AS A TABLE CLOTH, OR DRAPED IN FRONT OF A PLATFORM

The flag cannot be made into or used as underclothes, bath and floor mats or any similarly demeaning application

IT IS NOT ALLOWED TO TOUCH THE GROUND OR FLOOR

It should never be depicted, displayed or flown upside down (flying a flag upside down is the traditional sign of surrender!)

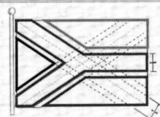

WHO THEY WERE..?
PEOPLE WHO HAVE PLACES NAMED AFTER THEM

Because of their life-changing roles in the struggle against apartheid, the 10 people described here all have public places named after them. The individuals represented experienced exile, life imprisonment, ostracism and even assassination. They helped form the ANC Youth League, the ANC Women's League, Umkhonto we Sizwe, the Pan Africanist Congress and the Progressive Federal Party. They endured the Sharpeville Massacre and the women's anti-pass march, and received honorary doctorates, awards and Nobel Peace Prize nominations.

WALTER SISULU NATIONAL BOTANICAL GARDEN

From humble beginnings in the Transkei, and a primary school education only, Walter Ulyate Max Sisulu rose to become an educated man and Deputy President of the unbanned African National Congress (ANC). During his political career he helped establish the youth wing of the ANC. He joined the South African Communist Party, thus cementing the relationship between the ANC and SACP, and was instrumental in transforming the ANC into a mass-based militant national organisation. Sisulu was married to Albertina for over 50 years. He died a few days before his 91st birthday on 5 May 2003.

OR TAMBO INTERNATIONAL AIRPORT

Oliver Reginald Tambo and Nelson Mandela ran the law firm Mandela and Tambo. Tambo helped form the ANC Youth League and served as its secretary. He was appointed Secretary General, then Deputy President and later President of the ANC. He helped draft the ANC Freedom Charter. His constitutional revision of the ANC became known as the Tambo Constitution. Tambo spent many years working for the ANC in exile, communicating to the world the situation in SA, and ultimately leading Umkhonto we Sizwe. Following the announcement of the 1985 State of Emergency, Tambo delivered a dramatic speech calling on people to 'render South Africa ungovernable.'

CHRIS HANI BARAGWANATH HOSPITAL

Martin Thembisile (Chris) Hani grew up a devout Christian, was exposed to Marxist ideology at university and obtained a BA degree in Latin and English. He was a member of the ANC Youth League, the SA Communist Party, and went into exile working for the ANC, Umkhonto we Sizwe. After the unbanning of the ANC, Hani returned to SA and became a charismatic and popular speaker in townships. His campaigning for the SACP helped his party prove a serious match for the ANC in the 1994 elections. However, in 1993 Hani was assassinated by Januzs Waluś, an anti-Communist Polish refugee. Conservative Party MP, Clive Derby-Lewis, was also implicated.

BRAM FISCHER INTERNATIONAL AIRPORT

Born into a prominent, conservative Afrikaans family, Abram and his wife Molly joined the Communist Party of South Africa (CPSA) in 1942. Despite his communist connections, Fischer continued practising as a lawyer. He was also a member of the Congress of Democrats and in 1953 was banned under the Suppression of Communism Act from most gatherings. Fischer led the defence team for the Rivonia accused (which included Mandela), helping obtain a sentence of life imprisonment rather than the death penalty. In 1966 Fischer was found guilty of violating the Suppression of Communism Act and conspiring to commit sabotage. He was sentenced to life imprisonment.

BEYERS NAUDÉ DR

Beyers Naudé, a former Broederbond member, studied theology and went into the ministry in the Dutch Reformed Church. In the early 1960s he became very conflicted regarding the church's support of apartheid, particularly after the 1960 Sharpeville Massacre. He helped found the non-racial Christian Institute and publicly condemned apartheid from the pulpit. As a result Naudé was completely ostracised by the Afrikaner community. He received several foreign awards and honorary doctorates that recognised his work in justice and peace, reconciliation and development, and race relations. Naudé succeeded Archbishop Tutu as the Secretary-General of the South African Council of Churches in 1985.

RUTH FIRST FREEWAY

Ruth Heloise First was a staunch communist and served as secretary of the Young Communists' League while studying at Wits. She became editor-in-chief of the left-wing newspaper, *The Guardian*, and was especially known for her exposé articles on labour conditions in the country. She was on the committee that drafted the Freedom Charter, attended Wits University with Nelson Mandela, and was married to Joe Slovo. First was born in Johannesburg in 1925 and was killed in Maputo by a letter bomb in 1982.

ROBERT SOBUKWE ST

Robert Mangaliso Sobukwe was a highly educated man. He joined the ANC Youth League while at university, and was an effective orator. Sceptical of the ANC's multi-racial path, Sobukwe was instrumental in initiating an African breakaway from the ANC which led to the birth of the Pan Africanist Congress (PAC). The PAC and Sobukwe launched a campaign on 21 March 1960 to protest against pass laws. On the same day, the police opened fire on other PAC protesters in what became known as the Sharpeville Massacre. Sobukwe was sentenced to prison, spent time in solitary confinement on Robben Island, and was subjected to years of house arrest.

HELEN SUZMAN BLVD

Helen Suzman entered politics in 1953, serving as a Member of Parliament for 36 years. She represented the United Party, then broke away to form the Progressive Party (which later became the Progressive Federal Party). The party had an openly liberal programme of extending rights to all South Africans with a qualified franchise. As the sole voice of SA's oppressed, Suzman publicly criticised the governing National Party's politics of apartheid at a time when this was unusual amongst White people. She served as president of the South African Institute of Race Relations, was awarded honorary doctorates for her anti-apartheid stance, and was nominated for the Nobel Peace Prize twice.

GOVAN MBEKI AVE

Govan Mbeki joined the South African Communist Party (SACP) in the 1950s and worked constantly to cement strong relations between the SACP, the ANC and the trade union movement. He was a leading pioneer in the founding of the people's army Umkhonto we Sizwe. Mbeki was sentenced to life imprisonment in the Rivonia Trial in 1964. On Robben Island, he published several books and articles, distinguishing himself as a great Marxist writer. In his scholarly work, he paid great attention to the application of the science and theory of Marxism to South African realities and conditions.

MOSES MABHIDA STADIUM

Moses Mncane Mabhida was a member of the ANC and the SA Communist Party and helped develop the South African Congress of Trade Unions (SACTU). In 1960 Mabhida began working in exile, representing SACTU, and then developing the ANC's armed wing Umkhonto we Sizwe. He was popular among ANC members and was a close friend of Oliver Tambo. Twenty years after dying in Maputo, Mabhida's embalmed remains were exhumed and repatriated to a liberated SA. In 2002, he was posthumously awarded the Order of the Baobab for his significant role in the liberation struggle.

HAYIBO!

Pronounced (haai-boh):

A Zulu and Xhosa word expressing disbelief or surprise
as in 'I don't believe what I am seeing' or 'no ways!'

HEALING FROM THE LAND

Africa is blessed with enormous biodiversity of which 5000 of the plant species are used for medicinal purposes.

Of the African biodiversity, these are just 10 of the more common medicinal plants that have received recognition internationally for treating and/or managing a wide variety of conditions.

Traditional medicine that has been adopted by other populations outside of its indigenous culture is termed 'complementary' or 'alternative' medicine.

African traditional medicine in its varied forms takes a holistic approach by involving both the body and the mind. The traditional healer typically diagnoses and treats the psychological basis of an illness before prescribing medicines, and particularly uses medicinal plants to treat the symptoms.

Source: Traditional Medicines in Africa: An Appraisal of Ten Potent African Medicinal Plants by M. Fawzi Mahomoodally.

SCELETIUM TORTUOSUM

This small groundcover plant is set to take the world of antidepressants by storm. For hundreds of years the indigenous people used *Sceletium tortuosum* as a mood enhancer, relaxant and empathogen. It is known by many names such as Kanna or Kougoed. Historically *Sceletium tortuosum* was chewed, smoked or used as snuff. Effects produced included euphoria and alertness which gently faded into relaxation. *Sceletium* has a mild anaesthetic effect in the mouth and was used by the San tribes if they were about to have a tooth extracted, or in minute doses for children with colic. Today *Sceletium* tablets are being used successfully around the world as a natural antidepressant by a number of psychiatrists, psychologists and doctors with excellent results as a safer alternative to other pharmaceuticals.

HONEYBUSH
CYCLOPIA GENISTOIDES

The leafy shoots and flowers of the indigenous *Cyclopia genistoides* are fermented and dried to prepare a tea which, since early times, has been used for its direct positive effects on the urinary system and its ability to aid weak digestion without affecting the heart. This tea contains no harmful substances such as caffeine. Over the past 100 years the tea has become a commercial product and is considered a health food.

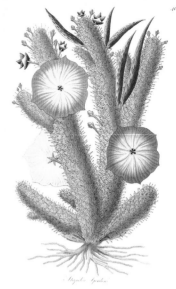

HOODIA GORDONII

The leafless succulent *Hoodia gordonii* grows in the Kalahari. The San people would nibble on Hoodia whilst hunting and could go without food for 24 hours in the harsh Kalahari Desert. It is known to maintain a high energy level and enhance moods. Independent tests conducted in England have proven its ability to curb the appetite and this native plant is now being exported and is in demand as a slimming agent.

UMCKALOABO
PELARGONIUM SIDOIDES

The tuberous *Pelargonium sidoides* is native to the coastal regions of South Africa. The root extract, also known as Umckaloabo, is a herbal remedy used in the treatment of acute respiratory infections. Numerous studies have shown its effectiveness in alleviating symptoms of acute rhinosinusitis and the common cold in adults.

BITTER ALOE OR CAPE ALOE
ALOE FEROX

Aloe ferox has a well-documented history and is depicted in San rock paintings. The bitter latex, known as Cape Aloe, is used as a laxative medicine and has antioxidant, anti-inflammatory, antimicrobial, and anticancer properties. The finished product has remained a key South African export product since 1761 when it was first exported to Europe.

DEVILS CLAW
HARPAGOPHYTUM PROCUMBENS

Harpagophytum procumbens is native to the red sand areas of the country and has been taken by San and Khoi peoples for millennia for multiple uses. The highly commercialised Devil's Claw has bulk exports mainly to Europe where it is made into a large number of health products such as teas, tablets, capsules, and topical gels and patches.

CENTELLA
CENTELLA ASIATICA

Known since prehistoric times, it is used for wound healing, burns, tuberculosis, skin diseases, eye diseases, fever, inflammation, asthma, hypertension, rheumatism, syphilis, epilepsy, diarrhoea, and mental illness. Today it is increasingly used in a combination of traditional and scientifically orientated medicine.

GUM ACACIA
ACACIA SENEGAL

Known for at least 4000 years, various parts of the plant are used to treat a wide number of infections such as bronchitis, diarrhoea, gonorrhoea, leprosy and upper respiratory tract infections. Western research has verified that Gum Acacia bark exhibits significant antibacterial activity.

ROOIBOS
ASPALATHUS LINEARIS

Endemic to South Africa, this fynbos species is cultivated to produce the globally popular herbal tea. It is lauded for its caffeine-free and comparatively low-tannin status with health-promoting properties, most notably its antioxidant activity. Recent research has confirmed its blood-pressure-lowering, antispasmodic, and bronchodilator effects.

BITTER MELON
MOMORDICA CHARANTIA

Momordica charantia, also known as Bitter Melon, is a tropical vegetable. The leaf may be made into a tea called 'cerassee'. The juice, extracted from the various Bitter melon plant parts, has a long history of use as a traditional hypoglycaemic agent for treating diabetes and the plant extract has been referred to as vegetable insulin.

Table Mountain was formally inaugurated in 2012 as one of the world's New 7 Wonders of Nature. Over 500 million votes from around the world were cast in the selection of the New 7 Wonders of Nature.

One of the world's 7 Wonders of Nature

Table Mountain National Park has more plant species in its 22 000 hectares than the British Isles or New Zealand have in their entire countries.

No place like home There is a 10 km² area on Table Mountain which is home to the world's rarest amphibian, the Table Mountain ghost frog. The frog is a critically endangered species and this area is the only place on Earth where it can be found.

Way back in 1856 Cape Town had its very own gold rush on the slopes of Table Mountain. The gold rush started when a servant of a Mr Salem was rumoured to have found a piece of gold-bearing ore. The Cape citizens swamped the mountain armed with picks, shovels and sieves. Mr Salem started selling food and refreshments at the base of the gorge, obviously at prices double those in town, and did a roaring trade. With time, people realised there was no gold and it later emerged that Mr Salem was an ex-convict from Van Diemens Land (Tasmania) and had lured the crowds using a piece of gold-bearing ore that originated from Australia!

Woodhead Dam, which is on top of Table Mountain, was built in 1897 with blocks of stone. Now over 110 years later this masonry marvel still supplies water to Cape Town. The American Society of Civil Engineers named it an 'International Historic Civil Engineering Landmark'. There are only 244 projects worldwide that have earned this prominent designation and these include the Washington Monument, the Eiffel Tower and the Sydney Harbour Bridge.

Table Mountain National Park, Western Cape

Where Stars

Photo courtesy of Michael Hammond, UCT

University World Rankings

There are 20 000 registered universities worldwide and there are 23 universities and universities of technology in South Africa. Research, involving 62 094 academics and 27 957 employers, taken globally revealed:

- All 23 South African universities rank in the top 50 % worldwide.
- Eleven South African universities rank in the top 7.5 % worldwide.
- UCT, Tukkies, Stellenbosch, Wits, Rhodes, UJ and UKZN are ranked in the top 3.5 % of universities in the world.

Unisa was the first dedicated distance education university in the world and with

Best Value in the World!

Source: Financial Times Global MBA Ranking 2015

The University of Cape Town's Graduate School of Business (GSB) is ranked the Top Business School in the World regarding value for money for its full-time MBA programme. This is calculated by the salary earned by alumni today, course length, fees and other costs including the opportunity costs of not working for the duration of the course.

TOP RANKING BUSINESS SCHOOL IN AFRICA

Source: Financial Times Executive Education rankings 2014

The University of Pretoria's Gordon Institute of Business Science (GIBS) is the **highest ranked African business school** and is ranked in the top 50 global schools in the world.

Triple 'Crown' Accreditation

Less than 0.5 % of business schools in the world received the triple 'crown' accreditation of AMBA (the Association of MBAs), European Quality Improvement System (EQUIS) and The Association to Advance Collegiate Schools of Business (AACSB).

Two of these are in South Africa:
- University of Stellenbosch Business School
- University of Cape Town Graduate School of Business.

FIRST MBA PROGRAMME

Outside of the United States, the first MBA programme was started by the University of Pretoria in 1949.

are made!

Graduates in the Labour Force

Source: South Africa @20 sagoodnews

In 1995: 460 000
In 2011: over a million

The unemployment rate amongst South African graduates is only **5.9%**

400 000 students is the largest open distance learning institution in Africa.

The University of Cape Town

The story of Tembi

I also wanted to contribute to society. I saw education as the key. Nothing was going to stop me.

At the age of 36, **Tembi Maloney Tichaawa** received a Doctorate in Philisophy from the University of KwaZulu-Natal. What makes his story so remarkable is that he started his life in South Africa in 1997 as a car guard with a big dream.

To pay his fees he worked in Cape Town as a car guard, then as a hotel security officer and night porter.

Tembi saved until he had enough to enrol at the Cape Peninsula University of Technology. After his degree he went on to complete a Master's degree cum laude and then his Doctorate in Philosophy. Now Tembi is a senior lecturer and director of the Centre of Excellence for Tourism Research at the Walter Sisulu University,

Tembi says he frequently chats to car guards telling them they are intelligent, young and vibrant and his message to them is not to feel sorry for themselves, to have a smile and to have a dream. But he says his job is not yet done as we need to work towards building a society which provides meaningful education.

Photo courtesy of Debbie Patching-Bozza

ROADSIDE LINGO

Whilst the rest of the world says traffic light, in SA we say robot.

The engine is under the bonnet,
a hood is what covers your head.
Your luggage goes in the boot,
a trunk is an elephant's nose.
The pavement is where pedestrians are
supposed to walk, and a sidewalk
happens after one too many beers!

ROAD CLOSED ➜
USE THAT BEHIND ROAD

Thank You For Your Patients

Need panel beating or a respray?

PENELBITING & RESBREY
0795702546

SORRY FOR THE INCONVENIENCE ERECTION GOING ON

ROAD IS TEMPORARY CLOSED FOR ERECTION

DETOUR USE THIS ENTRANCE ROAD CLOSED

In South Africa we don't drive on the left of the road, we drive on *what is left* of the road!

RULES OF THE ROAD

ELSEWHERE

Drive ➡

Drive slower ➡

Stop ➡

IN SOUTH AFRICA

⬅ Drive

⬅ Drive faster

⬅ Check for traffic cop, THEN GO!

IM NOT DRUNK ...JUST AVOIDING POTHOLES

KIA MOTORS

CEO

FISHING THROUGH THE AGES

Blessed with a coastline almost 3000 kilometres long and a landmass with numerous dams, lakes, rivers and streams South Africa has plenty to offer the fishing enthusiast. From game fish in two oceans to trout in mountain streams, there is something to challenge and entertain everyone. Many of South Africa's prime fishing spots offer not only good fishing but also include some of the most beautiful places in a country endowed by Mother Nature.

FROM GENERATION TO GENERATION

On the shores of Kosi Bay, life takes on a different meaning. The traditional fish traps or kraals have been used for survival for some 700 years. This way of fishing has been passed down from generation to generation by the local Tsonga people. Because the traps are small, similar to reed baskets, there's no major impact on the thriving fish population. Monitoring by locals, patient negotiation with local tribal authorities, and counselling local fishermen ensures this method of fishing is sustainable. Fish trapping remains a popular means of fishing for the locals and a marked and sustained increase in the number of traps has occurred, with more than a doubling in numbers between 1994 and 2000.

Photos courtesy of Marna Cilliers, Green Vision Foundation

LEARNING FROM THE KHOISAN

The fish traps in Stilbaai were originally built around 3000 years ago by the Khoisan. Although they were used by the Stone Age people, the fish traps are still in use today. Early cave dwellers noticed that fish got caught in the natural tidal pools as the tide receded. Enlarging these pools by packing stone in strategic areas enabled the fish to be caught by hand when the tide ran out. Packing the walls of the fish trap is a precise job and today only a handful of men are capable of doing it. More than 20 of these ponds are still maintained along the shore about half an hour's walk from Stilheuwels.

WEST COAST WAY OF LIFE

Generations of fishermen have made the sea their livelihood along the West Coast in towns such as Lambert's Bay, Paternoster, Saldanha and Langebaan. Although snoek is the most common species offshore, shore anglers are likely to find kabeljou, elf and yellowtail, as well as sharks and rays. The jumping thresher shark promises a good fight, as do larger skate.

AN UNUSUAL EXPORT

Fly fishing is a popular pastime, particularly in the KwaZulu-Natal Midlands, Mpumulanga province, and the Eastern Cape. In 1890 a cargo of 32 000 trout ova were sent from Scotland. The ova were released on the Boschfontein farm near Balgowan. They were hatched in water which was cooled each day with 500 pounds of ice. About 1500 trout fry survived to become the first trout in South African rivers. In 2003 heat-resistant trout, which can tolerate warmer conditions prevailing in Europe, were exported from South Africa.

BEACH VEHICLE BANNING

Coastal dune conservation in South Africa kicked forward a gear in 2001 when driving on the beaches was banned. This helped safeguard sensitive coastal birds whose nests were often crushed or their breeding season interrupted by vehicles. Studies found that birds were breeding earlier in the season and more successfully than they were before the 4x4 vehicle ban. When the 4x4 policy was reviewed, it was considered such a success that it is now set in stone.

Photo courtesy of Renier Nortje

The Constitution affords everyone the right to FREEDOM OF CONSCIENCE, RELIGION, THOUGHT, BELIEF AND OPINION.

THE CHALLENGES OF THE MISSIONARIES

Dr David Livingstone, the legendary missionary, was frustrated by the progress of their missionary work in the 1800's. The beliefs of the Setswana people, together with the Setswana-English language barrier complicated an already difficult situation. Max du Preez writes how the translation of English to Setswana posed some strange and hilarious results. In Setswana there is no word for 'spirit', the closest word means 'vapours rising from a boiling pot'. The language also does not differentiate between brotherly/godly love and physical/sexual love. The concept the Christian 'life after death' and Christ's resurrection also caused some alarm and confusion. It's no wonder a Livingstone sermon was interpreted as follows:

'That the God who lives in the ground will come down from the sky, accompanied by all the dead warriors that you have killed in battle. He will then proceed to have sex with everybody because the people have cow dung on the vapours of their boiling pots.'

The **'City of Saints'** is the name given to Grahamstown due to the number of religious buildings and the vibrancy of evangelism during its heyday.

The **first Hindu Temple** in Durban [and indeed Africa] was built on the banks of the Umbilo River in 1875 but was washed away by floods. A larger building, known as the Second River Temple, was later constructed in Bellair Road. It was declared a national monument in 1980 and is still in use today. South Africa has the largest concentration of Hindus in Africa.

At the 2001 census around 80 % of South Africans considered themselves as Christians. The 2011 census, however, did not include any questions on religion due to low priority. In a recent international study, the *Win-Gallup International Religiosity and Atheism Index* reported that **'religious South Africans dropped from 83 % of the population in 2005 to 64 % in 2012.'**

The **Nan Hua Temple** in Bronkhorstspruit is the largest Buddhist temple and seminary in both Africa and in the southern hemisphere.

The **Nizamiye Turkish Masjid** in Midrand, with its awe-inspiring dome and soaring minarets, is the largest of its kind in the southern hemisphere.

The **ZCC** (Zionist Christian Church) identified by a Dove or Star emblem have a strict code of discipline and its members are known in the community as peaceful, dependable and trustworthy.

Over three million of their estimated eight million supporters make the annual pilgrimage to Mount Moria every year. Their faith is a unique blend of Christianity and African traditional beliefs and they constitute the largest religious sect in southern Africa.

"The God who existed before any religion counts on you to make the oneness of the human family known and celebrated. "

- Desmond Tutu

THE WORLD AT WAR

-WWI-

THE FIRST WORLD WAR BEGAN IN 1914 AND LASTED UNTIL 1918. Three months into the war South Africa entered on the side of the Allied Forces. Altogether, 146 000 Whites, 83 000 Blacks and 2000 Coloureds volunteered for service in the South African Army.

During this time, the country was still recovering from the effects of the Anglo-Boer War which had occurred 14 years before. It is interesting to note that many of the South African soldiers who fought side by side in the trenches of WWI had fought against each other in the Anglo-Boer War. The First World War resulted in the **deaths of 7000** South Africans and a further **12 000 were wounded**.

FIELD MARSHAL OF PEACE

A former Boer leader, in the First World War Jan Smuts led the South African forces, capturing South West Africa from the Germans. He then commanded the British Army in East Africa. From 1917 to 1919 he was a member of the British War Cabinet and contributed to the formation of the Royal Air Force. He was a prime mover in setting up the League of Nations in the hope of preserving peace after the war. During the Second World War he was made a Field Marshall and served in Winston Churchill's Imperial War Cabinet. Smuts was the only person to sign the peace treaties that ended both the First and the Second World Wars.

THE SINKING OF *SS MENDI*

'Be quiet and calm, my countrymen. What is happening now is what you came to do … you are going to die, but that is what you came to do. Brothers, we are drilling the death drill. I, a Xhosa, say you are my brothers … Swazis, Pondos, Basotho … so let us die like brothers. We are the sons of Africa. Raise your war cries, brothers, for though they made us leave our assegaais in the kraal, our voices are left with our bodies.'

These are thought to be the last words of Rev Wauchope Dyobha just before the sinking of the SS Mendi. The tragedy struck in the early hours of February 1917. Whilst crossing the English Channel on its way to France , the *SS Mendi* collided with another ship, the *SS Darro*, which was travelling at full speed without any warning signals. The force of the impact was so great that it cut the *SS Mendi* almost in half, causing it to sink. A total of 616 South African lives were lost.

DELVILLE WOOD

One of the most famous battles occured in 1916 in 'Delville Wood', France. The SA Infantry Brigade was ordered to clear the wood of enemy soldiers at d'Elville, near the village of Longueal, France. The South Africans occupied the wood and were given orders to hold the fort 'at all costs'. Despite fierce counter attacks and artillery bombardments from German divisions, the South African brigade refused to surrender. After six days of ferocious fighting, the brigade was relieved. Of the 3 433 soldiers, only 750 remained - the rest had been either killed or wounded. The Battle of Delville Wood went down in the history of WWI as an example of supreme sacrifice and heroism. It remained the most costly action the South African Brigade fought on the Western Front.

Photo ©Amanda Slater

-WWII-

The Second World War began when Great Britain declared war on Germany on 3 September 1939. As an ally of Britain, South Africa followed suit two days later, then declared war on Italy in June 1940. When the United States entered the war after the Japanese attack on **PEARL HARBOUR**, South Africa declared war on Japan in December 1941. The South African Army and Air Force played a major role in defeating the Italian forces during the 1940-1941 East African Campaign as well as in battles against the Germans in North Africa before advancing into Italy itself in 1944-1945. Another important victory that the South Africans participated in was the liberation of Malagasy (today known as Madagascar) from the control of the Vichy French who were allies of the Nazis.

One of the lesser known incidents of the South African **6TH ARMOURED DIVISION** is their victory over the Nazi SS troops who massacred the inhabitants of the small town of Marzabotto. The Italian town named a road after the 6th Armoured Division and honours their liberation by hoisting the South African flag every year.

THE GREAT ESCAPE

The 'Great Escape' is a famous escape story of WWII. So famous, in fact, that a movie was made about it. Hundreds of prisoners of war in the Nazi camp in Poland dug three tunnels through which **76 airmen escaped**. The escape was led and organised by South African RAF pilot Roger Bushell whose father was the manager of one of the gold mines on the Rand, east of Johannesburg.

WARTIME HERO - JOB MASEGO

As a South African delivery worker, Job Masego read about the start of World War II in the newspaper. He joined the war and was posted to Egypt with the 2nd South African Division. It was here that he was captured and placed in a **prisoner of war camp**. While there, he found a cartridge buried in the sand. He continued searching through the sand and over time managed to uncover about 40 cartridges. Using the cordite contained in the cartridges together with a milk tin and pieces of fuse he had found, he managed to **make a bomb**. Sometime later, when Job and a number of prisoners were taken to a single-funelled ship anchored in the bay, his opportunity came. He snuck into the hold of the ship, put straw over the milk tin and soaked it in petrol. Back at his camp Job and the other prisoners sat watching and waiting. Black smoke began bellowing from the ship followed by a sheet of flame and a massive explosion. The ship had been destroyed. A few nights later Lance corporal Job Masego and fellow prisoner Private Masiya crept under the wire fence of their camp and escaped. Job Masego was later awarded the **Military Medal** for his bravery.

MOTHS - A WORLDWIDE ORGANISATION

The Memorable Order of the Tin Hats (MOTHS) was inspired by Natal Mercury cartoonist Charles Evenden. The movement was formed in 1927 to remember the servicemen who had given their lives in WW I and to help war veterans in need. Over 3000 men attended the first march through Durban and the movement spread rapidly around the world. It is still active today for service personnel in more recent fighting.

Cave Rock - Durban

WORLD WAR FORTRESS FOR MILLIONS

Cave Rock, as it is known today, is about 5 km south of the original cave rock on the Bluff. The original rock formed part of the end of the Bluff headland - making Durban easily identifiable to foreign enemies. In order to protect Durban's identity during World War II the rock was blown up and no longer exists today. During World War II the Bluff was transformed into a fortress. Durban took on the role of the southern hemisphere base port and provided services and refreshments for millions of servicemen and women and almost 200 000 ships.

Cave Rock illustration courtesy of Allan Jackson

THE SINGING LADY IN DURBAN

PERLA SIEDLE GIBSON, or the Lady in White, was a South African soprano who became famous during the Second World War for singing the troops in and out of Durban harbour. She could be spotted at the mouth of Durban Bay dressed all in white with a red hat. Using a megaphone she sang to over 5000 ships during the war and before long she was known internationally amongst the soldiers.

Information source: www.henrileriche.com

NATIONAL WOMEN'S DAY

August 9 is the day we celebrate the great achievements of South African women.

On this day in 1956, 20 000 women of all races from around the country marched to the Union Buildings in Pretoria, protesting against the government requirement for African women to carry passes. The march was led by the power team of Helen Joseph, Lilian Ngoyi, Albertina Sisulu and Sophia Williams-De Bruyn. They stood in silent protest for 30 minutes waiting for the petition - which contained 100 000 signatures - to be delivered to the Prime Minister's office.

Although an appointment had been made to hand the document over to then Prime Minister J.G. Strijdom, it was later announced that he would not see the women. They sang in anger:

'Now you have touched the women, you have struck a rock.'

To date, this is the biggest mass gathering of women ever held in South Africa. The women's anti-pass campaign lasted for seven years. Through constant arrests and intimidation, the apartheid government finally forced Black women to carry the passes and in the early 1960s, it put a total ban on all rural women coming to urban areas.

Today, although pass books are a thing of the past, this day is about honouring the history of women's resistance in South Africa. National Women's Day is a day to recognise the important role of women in the transformation to a democratic South Africa. Furthermore, it is also a day to celebrate and honour women and acknowledge that they should be treated with dignity and appreciation.

Malibongwe Drive in Johannesburg was named in honour of the women who marched in 1956.

Malibongwe means:
'Let them be praised.'

Photo © Lucian Coman

'Greatness is determined by service and nobody knows that more than South African women.'

— Oprah Winfrey

Over the years South African women have achieved great things. These are a few who have made a difference:

LILIAN NGOYI

Lilian was president of the ANC Women's League and the first woman to serve on the executive committee for the ANC. She also helped launch the Federation of South African Women, leading a march on 9th August 1956 to protest against women having to carry passbooks, which is commemorated today as Women's Day.

FATIMA MEER

Fatima helped to establish the Durban District Women's League - aimed at building unity between Africans and Indians - and was also a founding member of the Federation of South African Women. Fatima protested against the mass detention of anti-apartheid activists and was recognised for her contributions with three different awards between 1975 and 1994.

HELEN JOSEPH

As a founding member of the Congress of Democrats, she also played a vital role in the emergence of the Federation of South African Women. As an anti-apartheid activist, she was given the ANC's highest award - the Isitwalandwe/Seaparankoe Medal - for her dedication to the struggle for freedom.

EMILY HOBHOUSE

During the Anglo-Boer War, Emily worked to change the living conditions of the British-administered concentration camps. She also started the South African Women and Children's Distress Fund and set up Boer home industries in order to teach South African women how to weave and spin.

THULI MADONSELA

Thuli was appointed as the Public Protector of South Africa by Jacob Zuma. *Time* Magazine named her one of the 100 Most Influential People in the World and in 2014 she was named as South African of the Year by African News Network 7.

'As an African woman, I've learnt the importance of self-definition and living purposefully. It's vital that every girl determines, as early as possible, who she is and what her contribution to humanity will be.'

— Thuli Madonsela

NKOSAZANA DLAMINI-ZUMA

Nkosazana has served as the Minister of Health, the Minister of Foreign Affairs and the Minister of Home Affairs. She put forward the Tobacco Control Act, prohibiting smoking in public areas and is responsible for altering the health system to allow poor people access to free, basic healthcare. She was also the first woman to lead the African Union Commission.

FERIAL HAFFAJEE

When appointed as editor of *Mail & Guardian* Newspaper at the age of 36, Ferial Haffajee was the first woman to edit a national mainstream newspaper in SA. She was voted one of *New African*'s 100 Most Influential Africans and is a member of the International Press Institute and World Editors' Forum.

Women's Rights

The first woman to vote in South Africa, Sydney Stent, cast her vote in the general election of 1920. She had been included on the voters' roll by mistake on account of the masculine sounding name.

• • •

White women were given the right to vote in 1930 but it was only in 1994 that Black women were given the right to vote.

• • •

A re-enactment of the march was staged in 2006 for its 50th anniversary and included many of the veterans from the original march.

EMANCIPATION · EMPOWERMENT · EQUALITY

SOUTH AFRICAN ROYALTY

• • • ◆ • ❂ • ◆ • • •

South Africa is a country rich in culture and history that for hundreds of years has been populated by various clans, language groups, and nations. The tribes, which all bring different traditions and languages, include the Zulu, Xhosa, Sotho, Tswana, Pedi, Venda, Ndebele, Tsonga, Pondo and Swati. The country has a total of 13 kingdoms, although some no longer hold royal status. The kingdoms contribute to the country's democracy whilst still honouring traditional leadership of the African people.

Kingdom VS Chiefdom

According to custom, there are three levels of traditional African leadership: Kingship, Chieftainship and Headmanship. Chiefdoms give rise to kingdoms which use the Chiefdom as an integral aspect of the enlarged political entity.

ANCIENT KINGDOMS

Archaeologists have found evidence of kingdoms dating back hundreds of years. The most renowned of these is Mapungubwe where an entire palace was found. Archaeologists have also excavated the tombs of an African King and Queen from a civilisation in the 16th century. Found in the northern area of the Kruger Park, the Thulamela Stone Citadel was occupied from 1250 to 1700 AD. Mapungubwe is now a World Heritage Site.

THE CURRENT RECOGNISED KINGDOMS:

◊ **abaThembu:** Eastern Cape
◊ **amaXhosa:** Eastern Cape
◊ **amaMpondo:** Eastern Cape
◊ **amaZulu:** KwaZulu-Natal
◊ **Bapedi ba Maroteng:** Limpopo
◊ **amaNdebele:** Mpumalanga
◊ **VhaVenda:** Limpopo

Modjadji the Rain Queen

The legend of Modjadji the Rain Queen originated in the 16th century and to this day there still reigns a queen over the rain forests of the Luvedo valley. The Modjadji or Rain Queen is a hereditary queen of the Balobedu in South Africa's Limpopo Province. The successor to the position of Rain Queen is matrilineal and is passed from the queen to her eldest daughter, since males never inherit the throne. Yet the true origin of the queen is in question and many versions have been told over the centuries. The Modjadji is believed to possess special powers and has the ability to control the clouds and rainfall. She is a highly respected and feared queen in Africa, not only because of her power to withhold and bestow rain, but also because of her feminine nature, the fairness of her skin and the secrets of her valley. The current Queen Modjadji dwells in the same area, in her kraal, representing the very essence and history of the Balobedu nation.

King Moshoeshoe I

The first King Moshoeshoe became chief of the Bamokoteli tribe in 1820. The praise poems of the king say that he is named for the sound of a razor as he 'sheared the beards of his enemies'. During the great upheavals of the Mfecane, Moshoeshoe united diverse groups of refugees to form the Basotho nation. In 1833 he met with Catholic missionaries from the Paris Evangelical Missionary Society whom he then invited to visit his stronghold at Thaba Bosiu. Moshoeshoe's contact with the Voortrekkers in 1836 led to many border disputes and eventually two battles with the British Forces, in which the Basotho warriors remained undefeated. The king did eventually submit to Queen Victoria's suzerainty. Moshoeshoe's great-great-grandson, Archbishop Emmanuel Mabathoana, became the first Black African bishop of the Roman Catholic Church in Southern Africa and reigned as Archbishop of what was then Basutoland from 1952. Another great-great-grandson of his went on to become the King of Lesotho, calling himself Moshoeshoe II.

British Colonial Rule

Following the British colonisation of the Cape and Natal regions and the defeat of the Orange Free State and the South African Republic (Transvaal), the Union of South Africa was formed in 1910 and this united all four regions. From this time on, effective power was exercised by a Prime Minister under a constitution which recognised the ultimate sovereignty of the British Crown. In 1960, however, the National Party government held a referendum among white voters and the following year the Republic of South Africa came into being with an elected State President replacing the British monarch. A reminder of British rule is still evident in a number of place names such as Queenstown (named after Queen Victoria), Prince Albert (her royal consort), and Port Alfred (her son).

King Shaka

A crucial turning point in Zulu history occurred during the reign of Shaka as king of the Zulus from 1816. Shaka was a mighty and fearsome warrior who united the disorganised clans into a single powerful tribe. He revolutionised his army's weaponry and military tactics, methods which left his enemies outflanked and confused. In 11 years he increased the number of his army from 1500 people to 50 000 warriors. After the death of his mother, Nandi, Shaka became increasingly paranoid and unpredictable. In 1828 Shaka was assassinated by his half-brothers, Dingaan and Mhlangana. Shaka may have been a bloodthirsty tyrant but he increased the power and glory of his tribe.

Today, the King of the Zulus mostly reigns only ceremonially. Although he writes no laws and enforces no actions, the Zulu King still holds sway over certain issues when he speaks out and is regarded as a powerful influence on the modern Zulu tribe.

Illustration courtesy of Alex Coutts

King Hintsa

Hintsa ka Khawuta, or 'Hintsa the Great', was the King of the Gcaleka people from the Xhosa nation from 1820 until his death in 1835. He ruled with great sagacity and skill despite the conflict around him. Although Hintsa did not instigate the Sixth Frontier War between the amaXhosa nation and the British, he gave permission for his General Maqoma to lead the Xhosa forces. The incursion became known as 'Hintsa's War' by the amaXhosa. Hintsa's cold-blooded and treacherous murder at the hands of the British authorities became the main feature of the war, causing a great deal of anger in the memories of the amaXhosa. Considered a martyr and a hero, Hintsa has a legacy that lives on in poems and bedtime stories, as well as in the great novel by S.E. Krune Mqhayi, *Ityala Lamawele* ('*The Case of Twins*'). In 1999 South Africa institutionalised the King Hintsa Bravery Award for leaders who live and act in the spirit of Hintsa ka Khawuta.

Wise Words

Proverbs from our African languages

Photo courtesy of Debbie Patching-Bozza

SISWATI

'Emehlo namabili ayabonisana'

TWO EYES HELP EACH OTHER.
(IF YOU HAVE PEOPLE TO HELP YOU, YOU MAKE
INFORMED DECISIONS.)

NORTHERN SOTHO

'Mukola kuzhika mambo a nsulo'

A RIVER RUNS DEEP BECAUSE OF ITS SOURCE.
(YOU SHOULD RESPECT YOUR PARENTS AND ELDERS
BECAUSE THEY ARE THE SOURCE OF YOUR LIFE.)

TSONGA

'Ndlopfu a yifi hi rimbambu rinwe'

AN ELEPHANT DOESN'T DIE
FROM JUST ONE BROKEN RIB.
(DON'T GIVE UP WHEN YOU ENCOUNTER
AN OBSTACLE, GET UP AND TRY AGAIN.)

Photo courtesy of Bunyapon

NDEBELE

'Ukufunda akupheli,
kupheli amalanga'

LEARNING NEVER ENDS, IT'S THE DAYS THAT END.

XHOSA

'Ucel' amehlo'

HE OR SHE IS ASKING FOR EYES.
(HE OR SHE IS LOOKING FOR ATTENTION.)

'Udl'ukudla kwamudla'

HE ATE THE FOOD THAT IN TURN ATE HIM.
(WHEN A PLEASURABLE ACTIVITY HAS
PAINFUL REPERCUSSIONS.)

ZULU

'Bo tsholwa bo tjhesa,
bo tsohe bo fodile'

SOTHO

IN TIME, TEMPERS COOL DOWN.
(A HEATED ARGUMENT EVENTUALLY SUBSIDES.)

Meet our ancestors

Little Foot, Mrs Ples and the Taung Child

LITTLE FOOT

One of our human ancestors, dubbed Little Foot, probably fell into the Silberberg Grotto of the Sterkfontein Caves some time between about 2 million and 3 million years ago. Little Foot did not manage to escape alive but long after its death became world famous. After being trapped in the caves, the Little Foot skeleton was buried and it eventually fossilised. In 1994 palaeoanthropologist Professor Ron Clarke found some foot bones by chance among a box of sundry fossils stored at the caves. He identified the foot bones as those belonging to an early hominid, *Australopithecus*. Clarke's assistants then went in search for the rest of the skeleton in the caves. When they found Little Foot's skeleton it was pretty much complete, from foot to head, including 32 teeth. This is one of the most momentous palaeoanthropological finds in Africa. This almost-complete early hominid skeleton has provided scientists with important insights into human evolution.

THE TAUNG CHILD

The Taung Child lived at least 3 million years ago in a place now called Taung, a village west of Kimberley in the Northern Cape. In 1924 men working in a quarry unearthed an unusual small skull. Almost by chance, it was sent to Dr Raymond Dart at Witwatersrand University, who recognised its significance. It had a mixture of apelike and humanlike features, but was more human than ape and Dr Dart named it – and the species – *Australopithecus africanus*, meaning 'southern ape of Africa'. It is more commonly known as the Taung Child.

MRS PLES

Mrs Ples lived in the area where the Sterkfontein caves are today. She became an instant celebrity and remains one of South Africa's most famous figures to this day. It seems, however, that the archaeologist had it wrong; Mrs Ples, it appears, is a 'Mr Ples'. Mr (or Mrs) Ples is an ancient hominid making her (or maybe him) one of our earliest human ancestors aged roughly 2.5 million years. When she was found by Robert Bloom in 1947, she was originally identified as the species *Plesianthropus transvaalensis*, which is where she gets her nickname. Bloom later identified Mrs Ples as *Australopithecus africanus*. You can visit her in the Transvaal Museum of Natural History in Pretoria.

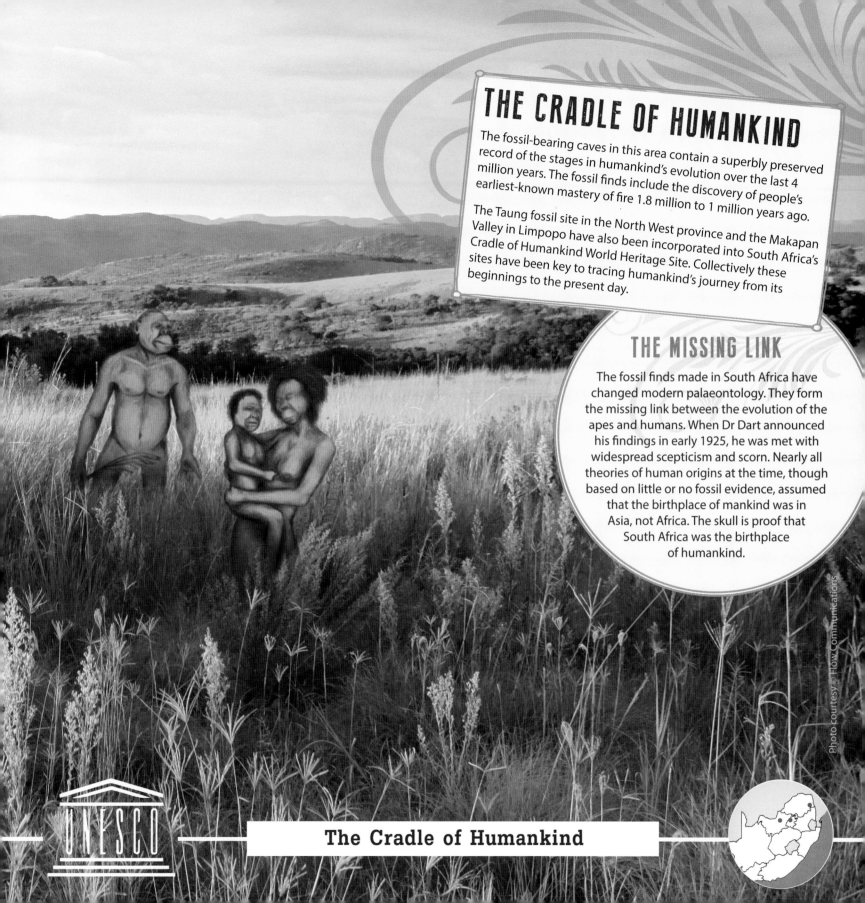

THE CRADLE OF HUMANKIND

The fossil-bearing caves in this area contain a superbly preserved record of the stages in humankind's evolution over the last 4 million years. The fossil finds include the discovery of people's earliest-known mastery of fire 1.8 million to 1 million years ago.

The Taung fossil site in the North West province and the Makapan Valley in Limpopo have also been incorporated into South Africa's Cradle of Humankind World Heritage Site. Collectively these sites have been key to tracing humankind's journey from its beginnings to the present day.

THE MISSING LINK

The fossil finds made in South Africa have changed modern palaeontology. They form the missing link between the evolution of the apes and humans. When Dr Dart announced his findings in early 1925, he was met with widespread scepticism and scorn. Nearly all theories of human origins at the time, though based on little or no fossil evidence, assumed that the birthplace of mankind was in Asia, not Africa. The skull is proof that South Africa was the birthplace of humankind.

UNESCO

The Cradle of Humankind

The Power of BOOKS

CLASSIC SA READS

Cry, The Beloved Country by Alan Paton
Long Walk to Freedom by Nelson Mandela
Country of My Skull by Antjie Krog
My Traitor's Heart by Rian Malan
Disgrace by JM Coetzee
Selected Stories by Nadine Gordimer
The Heart of Redness by Zakes Mda
Mafeking Road and Other Stories by Herman Charles Bosman
Fools and Other Stories by Njabulo Ndebele
A Dry White Season by André Brink

We should never underestimate the power of books to tell a story. Perhaps the most famous novel to come out of South Africa is **Alan Paton's** *Cry, The Beloved Country*. This 1948 work brought to the notice of the world the dilemmas of ordinary South Africans living under the oppressive system of apartheid.

> If you wrote a novel in South Africa which didn't concern the central issues, it wouldn't be worth publishing.
> — Alan Paton

SHAKESPEARE CONTENDER

After Shakespeare, **Athol Fugard** is said to be the playwright with the most plays performed in the world. This playwright, actor and novelist is world famous for his cutting portrayal of apartheid. In 2011 Fugard received a Tony Award for Lifetime Achievement in Theatre from the world's most prestigious theatre community. He is an Honorary Fellow of the Royal Society of Literature. The movie *Tsotsi*, which is adapted from the novel written by Fugard, won an Academy Award in 2005.

SOUTH AFRICA'S MOST LAUDED

JM Coetzee is one of South Africa's most lauded writers and is the most internationally acclaimed writer SA has produced. He is the winner of numerous awards including the Booker Prize in Britain on two separate occasions. A film of his book *Disgrace* won the International Critics' Award at the Toronto Film Festival.

Coetzee was awarded the Nobel Prize for Literature in 2003 and the Order of Mapungubwe by the South African government in 2005 for his 'exceptional contribution in the field of literature and for putting South Africa on the world stage.'

CRIME IN AFRIKAANS

Deon Meyer's crime novels have brought thrills and suspense to the South African literature market. Since his first novel in 1994, Deon's Afrikaans novels have been translated into 27 languages. He was the first South African to receive the Deutsche Krimi Preis. It is regarded as one of the oldest and most coveted German literary awards for crime literature.

SATIRE FROM THE PRISON CELLS

Herman Charles Bosman spent four years in prison for killing his step-brother, in what he called an accident. During this time he wrote his earlier novels, Many years later he wrote one of his best works, the traumatic yet humorous, *Cold Stone Jug*. Published in 1949 the book rose to classic status.

FOUNDING SA TEXT

Olive Schreiner's novel *The Story of an African Farm*, published in 1883 under the pseudonym Ralph Iron, won international recognition as the first realistic description of life in South Africa. Schreiner was an outspoken advocate of feminism, socialism, pacifism, and a critic of European imperialism.

AFRIKANER BANNED

André Brink was the first author to have his Afrikaans works banned by the SA government in 1973. His book *Kennis van die Aand* (now translated into English as *Looking on Darkness*) tells the story of a love affair between a Coloured man and a White woman during apartheid. Twice shortlisted for the Booker prize, recipient of the Martin Luther King Memorial prize and other international awards. In 1992 Brink was made Commandeur de l'Ordres des Arts et de Lettres in France.

FOUNDING BLACK LITERATURE

Viewed as the founding father of Black literature, **Sol Plaatje** wrote the first novel by a Black South African. *Mhudi* is an epic story set around the military encounters between the Tswana people and the Zulus. Plaatje also wrote a diary of the siege of Mafeking during the Boer War and translated four Shakespeare plays into Setswana.

AFRICAN ACCLAIM

An influential Black African writer, **Njabulo Ndebele** is an academic and a writer. In 1984 his publication *Fools and Other Stories* won the Noma Award, Africa's highest literary award for the best book published in that year. In 2004 he published *The Cry of Winnie Mandela* to critical acclaim.

BIRTHPLACE OF THE HOBBIT

JR Tolkien, author of the hugely popular *The Hobbit* and *The Lord of the Rings* trilogy, was born in Bloemfontein.

RACY, AGITATED, IMPRESSIONISTS

The writers for the popular *Drum magazine* (such as **Es'kia Mphahlele** and **Oswald Mtshali**) in the 1950s depicted a vibrant urban Black culture replete with jazz, shebeens and gangsters. The magazine served as a platform that revolutionised the writing of a new generation of writers who wrote about the conditions of their lives in their own voices and with a distinctive stamp and style.

CONFESSIONS OF AN ALBINO TERRORIST

Breyten Breytenbach was a vocal critic of apartheid. When he returned from exile in 1975, he was imprisoned for seven years for high treason. During this time he wrote his extraordinary prison memoir *True Confessions of an Albino Terrorist*. Breytenbach, critics noted, existed in the blind spot of apartheid South African society: the anti-apartheid Afrikaner, the 'albino terrorist'.

WORLD'S BEST SELLER

Wilbur Smith's novels are filled with romance and conflict set against the hunting and mining way of life in South Africa. He has sold more than 120 million copies and his books can fill Wembley Stadium twice over.

> Truth isn't always beauty, but the hunger for it is. – Nadine Gordimer

THE WORLD TAKES NOTE

Alfred Nobel described **Nadine Gordimer** as 'a very great benefit to humanity.' She was an influential writer and political activist and won the Nobel Prize for Literature in 1991. She was the first South African to win the award and the first woman to win in 25 years. Many of Gordimer's works were banned during apartheid; she nevertheless refused to go into exile.

COMMONWEALTH PRIZE

Successful playwright, novelist and poet, **Zakes Mda**, has won a number of awards in SA, the USA and Italy, including the Amstel Playwright of the Year Award, the Commonwealth Writers Prize for Africa, and the Order of Ikhamanga, in Bronze. As a member of the board of the African Writers Trust, Mda promotes the sharing of skills and resources amongst enthusiastic African writers.

MODERN DAY BEST SELLER

John van de Ruit is well known for the best-selling series of *Spud* books. His novels became an instant success amongst adults and children alike. The movies based on the Spud books have starred famous actor John Cleese and have been hugely successful.

AWARD-WINNING SCIENCE FICTION

Modern writer **Lauren Beukes** is proof that South African literature is not all about apartheid and historical struggles. Beukes's book, *Zoo City*, set in Johannesburg, won the UK's top science fiction prize, the Aurthur C Clarke Award in 2011.

LIVING THE STORY

Gcina Mhlophe, is not only a successful author but also a much-loved political activist, actor and storyteller who keeps history and culture alive. She works tirelessly to encourage children to read through storytelling. She performs in English, Afrikaans, isiZulu and isiXhosa! Witnessing Gcina's storytelling is an exceptional treat and a must for all South Africans.

UBUNTU

Ubuntu means humanness,
the ideal of being human.

DEFINITION OF UBUNTU

Ubuntu is a comprehensive, ancient African worldview based on the values of intense humanness, namely; caring, sharing, respect, compassion, and associated values, ensuring a happy and qualitative community life in the spirit of family.

ROUTE 62
WESTERN CAPE
TOURISM 62

Enjoy the rest of your journey! Liesje
Love, Daneel Jack

The story of the Ubuntu Girl

Sonja Kruse quit her job, gave her car away and left the familiar behind, to embark on a year-long journey across South Africa. Her mission was to demonstrate that Ubuntu was alive in the country. She became known as 'The Ubuntu Girl'.

With little more than a backpack, R100 and a deep belief that she 'is because of others', Sonja embarked on a journey of discovery. A journey of facing fears, preconceived ideas and changing perceptions that would reveal the sincere hospitality offered by complete strangers.

Along her unplanned route, 150 families from 16 different cultures opened their homes and hearts to this complete stranger. She stayed in affluent suburbs and dusty townships, in shacks and in mansions. She met pensioners, schoolchildren, farmers and labourers, rich businessmen, poor widows, housewives, truckers and curio sellers.

Sonja's wondrous journey tells the story of the remarkable people she encountered along the way. From her first night spent in the home of a Scenery Park mother who slept on the floor so that her guest could sleep in her bed, to

meeting the only White induna in the history of the Zulu Royal House on her last day. What these people all had in common was the spirit of Ubuntu, that compelled total strangers to reach out to a lonely traveller.

There were times when Sonja's faith in her journey of healing waivered. She experienced fatigue, isolation and an inability at times to humble herself, to be vulnerable and to ask for help. The scary moments were few, overshadowed by moments such as; inoculating cattle, making Umqombothi beer, removing alien plants on a fynbos farm and dancing in a Xibelani skirt. Sonja's journey was filled with extraordinary stories that taught her about humility and grace.

The story of the Ubuntu girl highlights the faith we have in one another. What Sonja learnt is that it's alright to question without the expectation of receiving an answer. If we can be honest about how little we know about one another then we can start to learn and grow together.

Photos courtesy of Sonja Kruse

Photo courtesty © Daryl Belfour, www.wildphotossafari.com

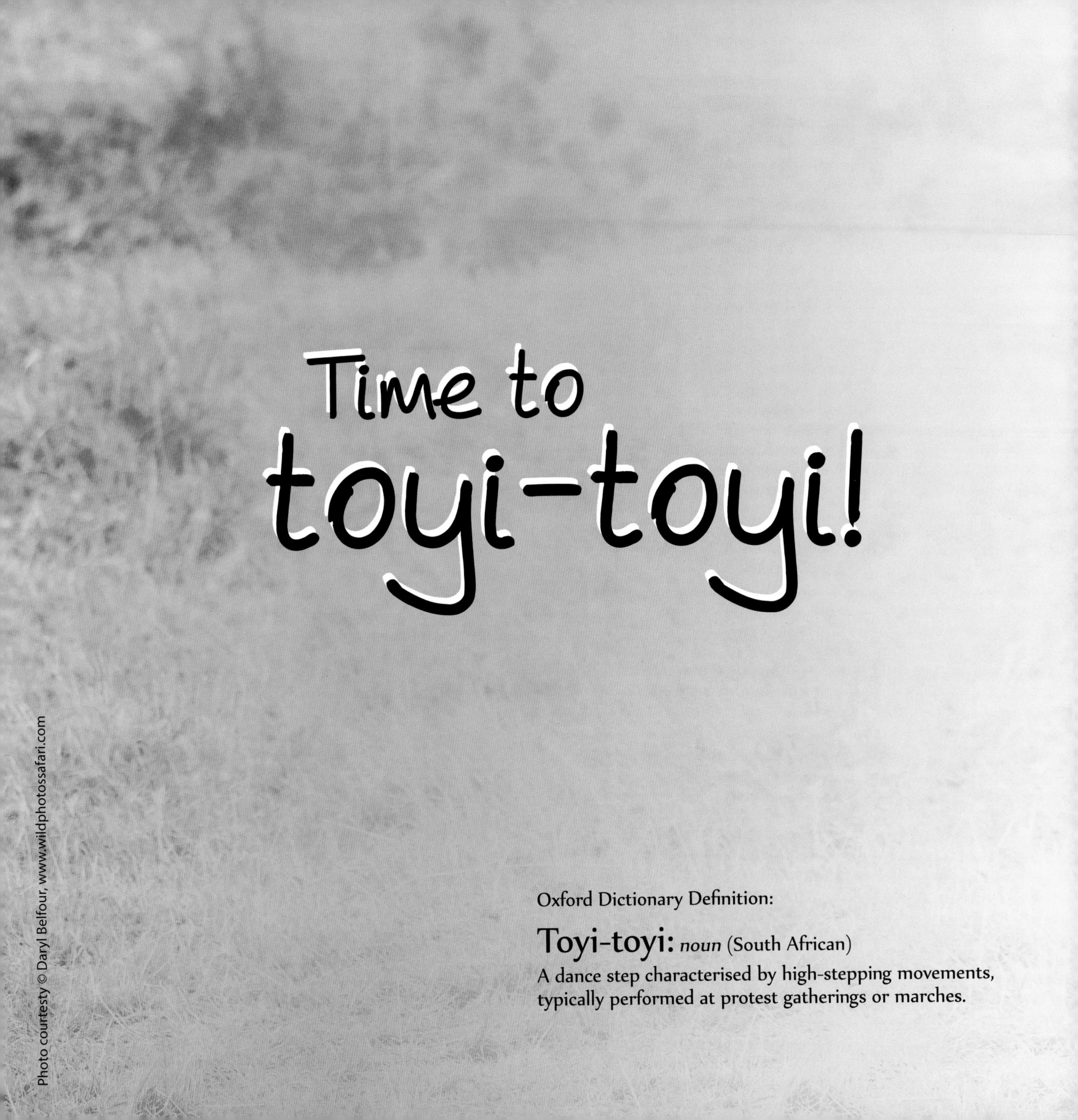

Time to toyi-toyi!

Oxford Dictionary Definition:

Toyi-toyi: *noun* (South African)
A dance step characterised by high-stepping movements, typically performed at protest gatherings or marches.

How well do you know your sport?

Which American stole the show at the 2013 Midmar Mile when he swam the race on both Saturday and Sunday? Clue: He was born without either arms or legs.

Which Olympic gold medallist was awarded Best Male Swimmer Overall at the FINA World Cup? Clue: He held four world records (for long and short course) in his discipline at the same time.

Who turned down an opportunity to play for Manchester United in favour of Italian club Lazio? Clue: He played for Pirates and was part of the SA team that won the African Champion Cup (CAF Champions league).

Who holds the record for the best bowling figures by a South African in an ODI when he took six wickets for 22 runs against Australia? Clue: He was the first Black player to play for the South African national cricket team.

Who is the only South-African-born tennis player to reach a Wimbledon final since the tournament joined the Open era? Clue: He played Boris Becker and Becker then went on to become the youngest player ever to win Wimbledon.

Which four-time world boxing champion gave his WBU Championship Belt to Nelson Mandela who, together with actor Will Smith, was watching him at the ringside? Clue: He was the shortest boxing world champion in the history of the sport.

Which tennis player broke Steffi Graf's winning streak of 45 matches and also handed Graf her worst-ever defeat, a 6-0, 6-1? Clue: She received three different awards by the WTA Tour, the most ever received by a single player in the history of the tour.

Who was nicknamed 'Road Warrior' because all of his 11 successful WBA title defences were fought on the road in countries around the world? Clue: When he retired, he was an undefeated champion and ranked the world's best super featherweight boxer.

Which athlete broke five world records and won a gold medal at the World Half Marathon Championship titles? Clue: When she competed in Barcelona in 1992 it was the first time South Africa had taken part in the Olympics in 32 years.

SPORTS QUIZ

 Which sportsman, together with Tim Noakes, co-founded the Sports Science Institute of South Africa and the UCT/MRC Research Unit for Exercise Science and Sports Medicine? Clue: He is also a member of the Laureus World Sports Academy.

 Which tennis player can claim victories over legendary tennis giants such as Andre Agassi, Stefan Edberg, Pat Cash, Björn Borg and John McEnroe? Clue: He was ranked world number one in the senior tour in singles and doubles.

 Which twelve-year-old became the youngest world record holder in the history of organised sport with a total of 17 world records? Clue: She was unable to win gold at the Olympics as South Africa was prohibited from participating in the games.

 Which golfer is one of only six golfers to twice win both the US Open and the Open Championship? Clue: He is the first player in history to win three successive titles in the one-on-one World Match Play Championship.

 Who was the first South African to compete in four successive Olympic games, won the FINA World Cup for two years in a row and won three gold medals? Clue: When he nearly drowned at the age of five, his parents sent him to water-safety classes.

 Which cricketer was the first Test batsman to make a hundred against each of the other nine Test nations? Clue: He also held the record for the highest score ever made in the Cricket World Cup (188 not out).

 Who had his record of 56 consecutive Grand Slam tennis tournaments equalled by Roger Federer in 2013? Clue: He won 6 of the 13 matches he played against Pete Sampras, one of the greatest tennis players of all time.

 Which sporting great was named after former Manchester United footballers, Bryan Robson and Gary Bailey? Clue: He was named the IRB World Player of the Year and shares the World Cup tournament record of eight tries.

Which Formula One World Champion was responsible for what is known as the worst crash in the history of the sport when he took out nine other cars? Clue: He drove for Ferrari team.

15. *Gary Kirsten*
16. *Wayne Ferreira*
17. *Bryan Gary Habana*
18. *Jody Scheckter*

SHIPWRECKS

Over the last 500 years hundreds of ships have been wrecked off South Africa's coasts. The Wild Coast, an area that stretches 250 km north of East London on the country's southeast coast, is notorious for its shipwrecking seas. Because of the danger to seafarers, the southwestern cape of the country was named the 'Cape of Storms' by Bartholomeu Dias, the first European known to have set foot on African soil. The oceans from these two coasts of the country (the warm Indian from the east and the cold Atlantic from the west) meet somewhere off Cape Point and this area is now home to over 140 shipwrecks. Roughly 1300 shipwrecks litter the entire South African coastline. Included here are some of the most interesting from the heroic to the ghostly, the historical to the mysterious, the groundbreaking to the infamous.

ATLANTIC OCEAN

HMS BIRKENHEAD:

Most Famous
Sank: 26 February 1852,
with the loss of 445 lives
Where: Near Cape Agulhas

Due to bad maintenance, most of the ship's lifeboats were not serviceable when the ship struck an uncharted rock. Thus only a third of the women and children on board were saved. All the nearly 500 British soldiers, bound for the 8th Frontier War, reputedly stood bravely in ranks and went down with the ship. This heroic act became known as the Birkenhead Drill, and, although its truth is disputed, was supposedly the origin of the phrase 'women and children first'. As a result of the disaster a lighthouse was erected at Danger Point in 1895.

JONGE THOMAS:

Most Heroic (Wolraad Woltemade)
Sank: 1 June 1773
Where: Salt River, Table Bay

When the *Jonge Thomas* was battered against jagged rocks while at anchor, passengers and sailors began falling into the raging sea; many drowned attempting to swim to shore. Wolraad Woltemade, passing by on horseback, swam out with his horse to the wreck. As he neared the ship he threw out a rope and made for shore, towing two men behind. Seven times he rode and swam out to the ship, rescuing 14 people. On his eighth trip, he and his horse were drowned when others, frantic in their efforts to be saved, grabbed hold of the animal and pulled both horse and rider under the waves. Woltemade immediately became a hero.

THE AMERSFOORT:

First Slave Ship to arrive at SA port
Arrived: 28 March 1658
Where: The Cape Colony

Although not recorded here as a shipwreck, it is worth noting the *Amersfoort*'s arrival at the Cape Colony with 170 slaves on board. The slaves were captured by the Dutch from a Portuguese slaver that was on its way to Brazil. Of the 250 slaves captured, only 170 survived their journey to the Cape. Most of the slaves on board the *Amersfoort* were originally captured by the Portuguese in, what is known today as, Angola.

THE FLYING DUTCHMAN:

A Ghostly Legend

No-one knows where or when the *Flying Dutchman* sank, although a famous sighting of this ghost ship occurred on 11 July 1881 off the Cape of Good Hope. It was sighted from the *RMS Bacchante* by a midshipman who later became King George V.

The captain of the *Flying Dutchman*, Hendric van der Decken, apparently ignored warning signs of bad weather. He continued round the Cape and, when a storm hit, he raised his fist and cursed God, swearing that he would continue even if it took him all eternity. It is said that from that day, the *Flying Dutchman* has been sailing the oceans trying in vain to make port.

'AN IMMENSE 'THING', ROLLING HELPLESSLY ABOUT IN THE OCEAN SWELLS. THE 'THING' LOOKED LIKE A GREAT OCEAN FISH. BUT IT HAD A FLAT TOP FROM WHICH STUMPS, LIKE TREE TRUNKS, PROTRUDED. LONG STRINGS WITH IMMENSE MATS WERE HANGING OVER THE SIDES AND TRAILING IN THE WATER. ALL DAY LONG THE MONSTER LAY WALLOWING, IMPELLED SHOREWARD BY THE SWELL. JUST AFTER SUNDOWN IT STRUCK WITH A CRASHING THUD AND THEREUPON, A LONG WAIL OF AGONY AROSE FROM THE PEOPLE ON IT. THEN IT REELED OVER SOMEWHAT AND APPEARED TO START TO MELT INTO THE SEA.'

This is how members of the Tshomane clan, who were living along the coastline of the Eastern Cape many years ago, described the first time they ever sighted a ship as related by Roger Webster in his *At the Fireside* series.

CAPE COLONY

INDIAN OCEAN

- Cape Vidal
- Wild Coast
- Coffee Bay
- Table Bay
- Cape of Good Hope
- Cape Agulhas

OCEANUS:
Worst Cruise Ship Disaster Video
(www.cruiselawnews.com)
Sank: 4 August 1991
Where: Coffee Bay

This Greek cruise liner sailing from Cape Town to Durban sank with 571 passengers and crew on board. Everyone survived. Cruise director and entertainers, and the South African Air Force, were credited with the rescue. Helicopter crews hoisted more than 170 passengers from the ship while South African Navy strike craft and private vessels rescued 400 more survivors from lifeboats. Captain Yiannis Avranas famously (or infamously) abandoned the ship while hundreds of passengers remained aboard saying he had 'gone ashore to re-establish communications'.

THE GROSVENOR:
Famous treasure ship
Sank: 4 August 1782
Where: Lwambazi Bay

As a result of faulty charts, the *Grosvenor* sailed into rocky shores and sank in deep waters off the Wild Coast. Over 100 people made it to shore but only 18 survivors reached the safety of the Dutch settlement at the Cape. Reputed to have been carrying a cargo of bullion, the *Grosvenor* wreck has yet to yield more than a few coins and artefacts. This is despite dozens of attempts at salvaging the ship's treasure.

SANTO ALBERTO:
First Major Journey of Discovery
Sank: 24 March 1593
Where: 16 km west of the Umtata River

After running aground off the Eastern Cape, the 125 sailors and 160 slaves on this Portuguese cargo ship decided to try to walk to safety at Sofala, 1 610 km away. And so began perhaps the first major journey of discovery through South Africa. On their way they traded with locals. Through amazing good fortune and fortitude, most of the original 125 arrived safely in Delagoa Bay 89 days later. Shipping disasters like these continued throughout the 17th century and some historians regard them as the main reason for the collapse of the Portuguese empire.

DOROTHEA:
A gold smuggling disaster
Sank: 31 January 1898
Where: 8 km from Cape Vidal

One of South Africa's most extraordinary shipwrecks occurred 8 km from Cape Vidal in early 1898. For no apparent reason the *Dorothea*, a wooded barque, was abandoned by her crew in perfectly calm weather. The crew was picked up by a passing steam ship but the *Dorothea* drifted to shore and sank. The ship was reputed to have been transporting the 'Kruger millions' or involved in gold smuggling (whether Oom Paul's or not). These rumours led to numerous salvage attempts. To date, no treasure has been found.

OOPS! WHAT were they thinking?

South Africans who were around in the '80s will remember when **CHRISTOPHER DINGLE,** who was the presenter of the TV programme *Midweek*, was the first person to say the 'f' word on television. While recording, he became agitated and blurted out the words 'Oh f***!'.

Then came the incident that shocked KwaZulu-Natal viewers in 1986. During the TV1 news, two technicians watching porn had to do a patch to the bulletin. But they unfortunately connected their sexy stuff directly through the switching feed and viewers were subjected to a 10-second insert of porn!

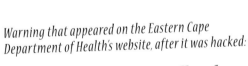
Warning that appeared on the Eastern Cape Department of Health's website, after it was hacked:

'The page performed an illegal operation and was promoted to vice-president.'

Alternative suggestions submitted by the public included:

'The page is sleeping. After all, this is African time we are talking about.'

'The page was considered redundant and was given a raise so it now works even less.'

'I LOVE AFRICA
IN GENERAL.
South Africa and
West Africa. they are
both great countries.'

Paris Hilton

Signed, Sealed and (Mis)Delivered

What a furore the Infamous sign language interpreter, **THAMSANQA JANTJIE** created. He was the official interpreter for the 2013 memorial service of the late former President, Nelson Mandela. What he had failed to disclose was that his sign language skills left a lot to be desired. In fact, one questions if he had any sign language skills at all. After the event the issue was featured on the *Jimmy Kimmel Live* show during which an expert sign language interpreter translated the tributes delivered by the various heads of state. An excerpt of what Jantjie actually signed goes as follows:

'I support basic salutations here, salutations. Inside, joining in this week's cigarette, inside to prove, and on and on, to support. I would please to say from me to you, talking to you so far.'

Watch this on YouTube!

> '*Where in the world is there a more just society today than South Africa?*'
>
> *PW Botha, Former Prime Minister of South Africa, 1976*

> '*I agree with everything I have just said.*'
>
> *Piet Koornhof, apartheid-era National Party cabinet minister*

> '*I never called him a liar. I said he was lying.*'
>
> *Prosecutor Gerrie Nel in his closing arguments in the trial of murder-accused paralympian Oscar Pistorius*

Watch this on YouTube!

The (unsung) song of our people

South Africans are as passionate about their rugby as they are about their country. Hence, the uproar when our treasured national anthem was blundered on two separate occasions by experienced South African musicians.

At a Springbok test match against France in 2009, **RAS DUMISANI** was poised to sing the national anthem in front of a global audience. His performance, which was broadcast to millions around the world, made headlines when his vocals sounded like two vervet monkeys fighting over the last marula. The camera close-up images of the team line-up started with the usual look of emotion and pride but quickly changed to confusion then horror and even to amusement as the anthem progressed.

The Just Jinja front man, **ARD MATTHEWS**, took the limelight in 2011 when he sang the anthem at a live broadcast of the Springbok squad-selection ceremony. Believe it or not he forgot the words.

Watch these on YouTube!

Simply offsides!

We love our sporting legends for their antics both during and after their matches, but we can't seem to shake off some of the ludicrous things that they sometimes say.

HERSCHELLE GIBBS, a noted cricketer and amnesiac, confessed at his book launch that he hadn't even read his own co-authored biography. He did, however, admit to reading 'most of it'.

'How high are we above sea level?' **JACQUES KALLIS**, a famous cricketing legend is infamous for having asked whilst jogging with the team along a beach in the Middle East.

Pieter de Villiers on South Africa's victory over the All Blacks:

'We went wild, wild, wild - some of the guys went wilder than that.'

Better left unsaid …

MISS TEEN SOUTH CAROLINA, LAUREN CAITLIN UPTON'S media frenzy started after she provided the strangest answer in the history of the Miss Teen USA pageant. Her beauty queen babble regarding South Africa went viral and led to a string of television appearances. If only she had taken Geography or simply stuck to 'world peace…'

The live TV interviewer asked the question: 'Recent polls have shown a fifth of Americans can't locate the US on a world map. Why do you think this is?'

And the Miss Teen contestant answered: 'I personally believe that US Americans are unable to do so because, um… some people out there in our nation don't have maps and, uh… I believe that our, uh… education like such as, uh… South Africa and, uh… the Iraq and everywhere like such as… and I believe that they should, uh… our education over here in the US should help the US, uh… should help South Africa and should help Iraq and the Asian countries, so we will be able to build up our future.'

SLAVE TRADE

SOUTH AFRICA'S COLONISATION MEANT THE INTRODUCTION OF SLAVES TO THIS COUNTRY. BROUGHT IN FOR LABOUR, SLAVES UNKNOWINGLY WENT ON TO ALTER OUR HISTORY FOREVER. TODAY, THEIR MARKS LIE IN OUR RICH HERITAGE, INHERITED NAMES AND FOOD, ARCHITECTURE AND ETHNIC GROUPS. SLAVERY ATROCITIES IN OTHER PARTS OF THE WORLD WERE OFTEN WORSE THAN THEY WERE HERE.

WHERE IT ALL BEGAN...

This gruesome tale began in 1658 in the Cape Colony when 170 slaves arrived in Table Bay aboard the *Amersfoort*. Mostly from Angola, these first slaves were originally from a Brazil-bound Portuguese slaver and over the years many shipments of slaves came from West and East Africa, Madagascar, India, Ceylon, Burma, Malaysia and Indonesia. The slaves had been brought in (mostly by Portuguese, Dutch and British colonisers) to provide a labour force. A booming trade meant that slaves soon outnumbered the settlers and by the time of the complete emancipation of slaves in 1838, the slave population stood at around 38 000. Although slave trading was abolished in 1808 it was only in 1834 that slave ownership and all forms of slavery were abolished in the British Empire. December 1, 1834 saw the Slavery Abolition Act implemented throughout the British colonies. Slaves were apprenticed to their owners for a few years thereafter, delaying actual freedom. However, slavery did effectively meet its end sooner in South Africa than elsewhere in the British Empire.

Image source: Inyathelo

A LIFE OF HARD LABOUR

The first Europeans to settle at the Cape were employees of the Dutch East India Company. The first shipload of slaves arrived six years later. At that time many company employees had been released from their contracts and given plots of land to farm. These 'free burghers' in turn purchased slaves. Slaves performed agricultural work on wine and wheat farms from 1658 onwards but also worked in the domestic sector, on salt pans and hunting seals. Some slaves were skilled builders, woodworkers, carvers, silversmiths, wainwrights, coopers and tailors. The results of this work are still evident today.

HERITAGE FROM SLAVERY DAYS

Many South Africans are direct descendants of slaves and are members of the *Coloured* community, as well as of a sub-group of the Coloured people known as *Griquas*. Many dishes eaten today are linked to our slave history like: sosaties, bobotie and bredies. Ornate handcrafted Cape furniture is a reminder of the skilled craftsmen who were slaves, and who also built many of the gabled Cape buildings in the style known as 'Cape Dutch'. The Slave Lodge in Cape Town is now a museum that represents the slave experience. Afrikaans evolved due to slavery and many Malay words are present in the language today. Islam, Hinduism and Catholicism were all introduced by Portuguese-captured slaves.

SLAVERY'S INHUMANITIES

Slaves led terribly harsh lives, working long hours. They were often badly fed and lived in dirty, crowded conditions. They had no rights or freedoms, and if they tried to escape they were severely punished. There were laws that were supposed to protect them, but slave owners often ignored these laws and subjected their slaves to terrible beatings, starvation and other cruelties. Although sex between the White men and slaves was forbidden, women were often raped by their owners. Slaves were not allowed to marry without their owner's permission, and if they had children these also became slaves. After the abolition of the slave trade owners began treating their slaves slightly better because they were unable to replace them, especially if the slaves were highly skilled or converted to Christianity. When slavery was finally abolished, many slaves decided to carry on working for their former owners.

CELEBRATING FREEDOM

The Cape Minstrel Carnival is Cape Town's longest-running street party. It dates back almost 200 years to the old slave traditions during the days of the Cape Colony.

Historically this is the one day of the year that the Cape slaves were given off. The day has been celebrated ever since with a spectacular parade of music and merrymaking as a confirmation of freedom. The local community dressed in flambouyant minstrel costumes with parasols, dance and sing from the former District Six through the city centre.

THE SLAVE DISTRICTS OF SOUTH AFRICA

The Slave Lodge in Cape Town (built in 1679) housed the slaves of the Dutch East India Company between 1679 and 1811. Although primarily designed as accommodation, the Lodge also operated as a busy brothel. Runaway slaves and communities that developed as a result of slavery settled on the slopes of Signal Hill in an area known as Bo-Kaap ('above the Cape'). Bo-Kaap slaves also lived in De Waterkant (next to Bo-Kaap) and Hangklip. After 1838, many 'free Blacks' lived in lower Cape Town and in the famous District Six. These areas became known for their cultural diversity as well as for the crafts and pastimes that slaves enjoyed whilst living there. Singing, dancing and the playing of musical instruments (in 'slave orchestras') was common in slave settlements.

'Our deepest fear is not that we are inadequate.
Our deepest fear is that we are powerful beyond measure...'

It is our light, not our darkness
That most frightens us.

We ask ourselves,
'Who am I to be brilliant, gorgeous, talented, fabulous?'
Actually, who are you not to be?
You are a child of God.

Your playing small
Does not serve the world.
There is nothing enlightened about shrinking
So that other people won't feel insecure around you.

We are all meant to shine,
As children do.
We were born to make manifest
The glory of God that is within us.

It's not just in some of us;
It's in everyone.

And as we let our own light shine,
We unconsciously give other people permission to do the same.
As we are liberated from our own fear,
Our presence automatically liberates others.

- This passage, from A Return to Love *by Marianne Williamson,*
was quoted by Nelson Mandela in his 1994 inaugural address.

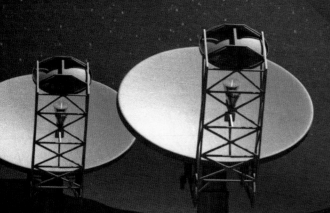

SALT is capable of detecting light in the universe a billion times too faint to be seen with the unaided eye. In layman's terms it is strong enough to see an image as faint as a candle flame on the moon.

[SALT]
AFRICA'S GIANT EYE ON THE UNIVERSE

The Southern African Large Telescope (SALT) in Sutherland is the largest single optical telescope in the southern hemisphere and among the largest in the world. It has a hexagonal primary mirror array 11 m across, comprising of 91 individual 1 m hexagonal mirrors.

SALT is situated on a mountain top 14 km out of the town of Sutherland (Northern Cape). Sutherland is one of the most geographically stable places on the planet and its night skies are among the world's clearest, making it one of the best star-viewing destinations this side of the equator. The telescope is overseen by the South African Astronomical Observatory (SAAO), a facility of the National Research Foundation (NRF).

[SANSA]
South African National Space Agency (SANSA) hosts the only Space Weather Regional Warning Centre in Africa and operates as part of the International Space Environment Service (ISES). SANSA's Space Weather Centre provides an important service to the nation by monitoring the Sun and its activity, providing space weather forecasts, warnings, alerts, and environmental data on space weather conditions.

[SKA TRIVIA]

✧ The data collected by the SKA in a single day would take nearly two million years to play back on an iPod.

✧ The SKA will use enough optical fibre to wrap twice around the Earth!

✧ The SKA central computer will have the processing power of about 100 million PCs.

✧ The aperture arrays in the SKA could produce more than 100 times the global Internet traffic.

✧ The SKA will be so sensitive that it will be able to detect an airport radar on a planet tens of light years away.

✧ KAT-7 is the precursor to MeerKAT. The latter was originally known as the Karoo Array Telescope (KAT). It was to consist of 20 receptors. However, when the South African government increased the budget to allow the building of 64 receptors, the team renamed it 'MeerKAT' - i.e. 'more of KAT'. The meerkat is a small animal of the mongoose family that lives in the Karoo.

[THE SKA PROJECT]

The Square Kilometre Array (SKA) project is an international effort to build the world's largest radio telescope, with a square kilometre (one million m²) of collecting area. SKA is not a single telescope, but a collection of thousands of radio telescopes called an 'array'. These telescopes will be spread over long distances and deployed in three unique configurations, enabling astronomers to monitor the sky in unprecedented detail and survey the entire sky thousands of times faster than any system currently in existence. SKA is in development in Australia and South Africa, with two complementary world-class instruments planned - one in Australia, one in South Africa.

Construction of phase one, MeerKAT, is currently being built in the Karoo. KAT-7 (the seven-dish MeerKAT precursor array) was completed in 2010 and has already delivered images of the Centaurus A, a galaxy 14 million light years away. Construction of the SKA is set to start in 2018, with early science observations scheduled for 2020.

TO INFINITY AND BEYOND...

[BUSHMEN] Long before these enormous scientific advancements into space, the Bushmen in this country were gazing at the stars.

According to the Bleeks, a father-and-daughter team in the Cape, the astronomical knowledge of the Bushmen was, well, astronomical. In the 1900s the Bleeks learnt the Bushman language and recorded some of their insights and legends. One such story retold by Roger Webster in his *At the Fireside: True South African Stories*, is called 'The Jewel of the Night.' This myth talks of a planet which they said rose in the morning and loved the Earth-Mother so much that he would look at her face six times, while she showed him her face but once. In addition, he would always be in the company of only one child. In 1930 Pluto was discovered by Europeans. This newly found planet, which was invisible to the naked eye, rotated on its axis six times faster than Earth – thereby showing its face six times to the Earth's once. In 1978 Pluto's single orbiting satellite was also discovered and named 'Charon'. This was what the Bushmen called the planet's 'one child'. These discoveries were just as the Bushman myth had described it, long before SKA and SALT were around.

WHERE IT ALL BEGAN

GONDWANA – THE LAND OF DINOSAURS

GONDWANALAND

Over 250 million years ago a major extinction event occurred which destroyed about 96 % of all existing species. The world's best example of the fossilised remains of the creatures that lived before this catastrophic event is found embedded in rocks in the Karoo.

The fossil of a Sauropod named Antetonitrus, dating from the Triassic Period, has been found in the Ladybrand District of the Free State. The world's oldest fossils of dinosaur nests, tightly clustered eggs, including magnificently preserved embryos of the Massospondylus, are found in the region of the Drakensberg. The near-perfect skeleton of an Aardonyx celestae, a seven-metre long dinosaur, is found in the area near Senekal of the northern Free State.

GONDWANA was the ancient supercontinent that incorporated present-day South America, Africa, Arabia, Madagascar, India, Australia and Antarctica. The rock strata that link South Africa to similar systems in India and in South America are called the Karoo System. It is in this rock that evidence of the dinosaurs which roamed the Earth can be found. In fact, South Africa has the most complete fossilised set of extinct animals in the world.

The landscape of Gondwana looked very different to what it does today. The region around what is now the Golden Gate area was semi-desert to true-desert conditions. The Massospondylus dinosaurs lived along the floodplains of the rivers that crossed this dune-covered desert. Each breeding season large numbers of Massospondylus returned to the area to lay their eggs and to raise their offspring. One day, 195-million years ago, a mother dinosaur laid a clutch of six eggs. Inside the eggs the tiny embryos grew to the point of hatching. One dinosaur chipped its way out of its egg, hatching into a harsh environment. The second hatchling was just emerging from its shell when it was smothered by a giant sandstorm. A third Massospondylus, still perfectly rolled in its egg and about to hatch, was also covered in the storm. Over millions of years the rivers dried up. The dust storms grew more regular as the desert moved in. And in time the Massospondylus genus and species went the way of the two embryos that had died before barely being hatched – eventually becoming extinct. These eggs and embryos were preserved for millions of years in the South African rock.

2 cm

JURASSIC: 200 - 145 MILLION YEARS AGO

CRETACEOUS: 145 - 66 MILLION YEARS AGO

The fossilised bones of the Nqwebasaurus, over 145 million years old, have been discovered in the Eastern Cape.

Finally, over 65 million years ago, a mass extinction event occurred destroying 70 % of species, including the dinosaurs.

A land with 2000 million

RICHTERSVELD – A cultural and botanical landscape

This world heritage site, which is roughly twice the size of Singapore, has a geological history that stretches back 2000 million years, almost half the life of the Earth. The Richtersveld National Park bears evidence of early human inhabitation which dates back to 2200 BC. This area sustains a group of the Khoikhoi named the Nama people. The Nama are pastoralists and live a semi-nomadic life with seasonal migrations and grazing grounds. Their homes are portable rush-mat houses. They collect medicinal and other plants and have a strong oral tradition associated with different places and attributes of the landscape.

years of history

Richtersveld National Park, Northern Cape

LETS DO LUNCH U BUY

Traffic Light Teacher

Zulu Words R1
+
Free Pronounciation

eg. Learn — funda

THE TRAFFIC LIGHT TEACHER

The story of Johannesburg's coolest entrepreneur went viral when the image *#trafficlightteacher* first appeared on the Internet. The publicity resulted in 'The Traffic Light Teacher' being awarded a bursary to study, thus enabling him to follow his dream.

MEET PHILANI DLADLA, THE PAVEMENT BOOKWORM.

www.pavementbookworm.co.za

Philani reviews and sells books for motorists while they wait for the traffic light. He has read all the books in his collection and sells them as a way to raise money for himself and some of his homeless friends.

PUTTING ON A ROAD SHOW!

I KEEP THIS INTER-SECTION SPOTLESS & CRIME FREE SPOT GOD BLESS U

I AM NOT SUAREZ I WONT BITE!

Photo: Facebook, Africa this is why I live here

WIFE KIDNAPPED BY NINJA NEED R10 FOR KARATE LESSON

Photo: source unknown

Photo courtesy: Lulamile Feni, Daily Dispatch

TEST YOUR

TRUE OR FALSE?

The South African comic book, *Supa Strikas*, is the world's biggest monthly comic book.

→ **TRUE:** There are 720 000 comics published monthly across Africa, in Latin America, Asia and Europe.

South Africa has one of the lowest divorce rates in the world.

→ **TRUE:** The divorce rate is ranked the sixth lowest in the world.

The 'brain drain' in South Africa is one of the highest in the world.

→ **FALSE:** South Africa is not even listed in the top 20 countries.

A racehorse can run twice as fast as a lion.

→ **FALSE:** A lion can run 75 km/h and a racehorse can run 69 km/h.

Cape Point near Cape Town is the most southerly point of Africa and the spot where the Atlantic and Indian Oceans meet.

→ **FALSE:** Cape Agulhas, 150 km east-south-east is the most southerly point and where the two oceans meet.

South Africa is ranked among the most representative in the world with respect to women in parliament.

→ **TRUE:** South Africa ranks as number five worldwide.

The first lighthouse to be built in South Africa was the Cape Point lighthouse in 1860.

→ **FALSE:** It was Green Point lighthouse in 1824.

South Africa has one of the ten longest railway networks in the world.

→ **TRUE:** SA has the sixth longest railway network in the world.

The Gariep Dam is the largest in South Africa and the Vaal Dam is the second largest.

→ **FALSE:** The Vanderkloof Dam has the second largest capacity followed by the Sterkfontein Dam and then the Vaal Dam.

South Africa has almost 80 % of the world's platinum reserves.

→ **FALSE:** South Africa has 88 % of the platinum-group metals.

The tallest trees in Africa are known as 'The Magoebaskloof Triplets'.

→ **TRUE:** These Eucalyptus Saligna trees are more than 80 metres tall.

KNOWLEDGE

Which airport in SA has one of the world's ten longest runways?

A) O.R. Tambo Int., Gauteng
B) King Shaka Int., KwaZulu-Natal
C) Port Elizabeth Int., Eastern Cape
D) Upington Airport, Northern Cape

Answer: D - Upington airport has a runway of 4 900 m. OR Tambo runway which is also considered to be amongst the longest in the world is 4 400 m.

South Africa's defence spending (in $bn) is higher than which of the following countries?

A) United Kingdom
B) Australia
C) Italy
D) None of the above

Answer: D - All these countries are ranked in the highest 15 countries worldwide. South Africa is not included in the top 15.

In the classic novel, *Sense and Sensibility* by Jane Austen, what does Mrs Jennings recommend for 'its healing powers on a disappointed heart?'

A) Constantia wine
B) Rooibos tea
C) Coca Cola
D) French champagne

Answer: A - Constantia wine.

On which line of latitude does Johannesburg lie?

A) 26.2044 °S
B) 5.9 °N
C) 45.1652 °N
D) 35.3728 °N
E) 45.02 °N

Answer: All of the above. There is a town called Johannesburg in California, Wisconsin, Michigan (all in the USA) and in Suriname.

If you built a flight of stairs to the bottom of the deepest mine in the world how many storeys would it be?

A) 1300 storeys
B) 1000 storeys
C) 750 storeys
D) 500 storeys

Answer: A - The TauTona gold mine, just outside Johannesburg, is the deepest mine in the world. It is 3900 m deep, equivalent to at least 1300 storeys.

Which is the only South African company to be listed on the Fortune 500 Top Global Companies?

A) Vodacom
B) ABSA
C) Sasol
D) MTN SA

Answer: D - MTN is number 188 on the list with a brand value of over R43 billion. The other top South African brands, in value order, are Vodacom (R19 billion), Sasol (R18 billion), Standard Bank (R14 billion) and ABSA (R12 billion).

Which flower appears on South African coins?

A) Strelitzia
B) Protea
C) Arum lily
D) All of the above

Answer: D - All of the above. Strelitzia 50c, King Protea 20c and Arum lily 10c.

Which is the largest port in SA?

A) Durban
B) Saldanha Bay
C) Port Elizabeth
D) Richards Bay

Answer: D - Richards Bay is the leading port in terms of cargo volume (84 937 million tons per year in 2010) and the biggest in terms of land and water area.

CAN YOU GUESS?

- Beer -

TRADITIONAL AFRICAN BEER

has been made for centuries and has numerous names in the various languages. Known as mahewu, mechow or umqombothi, this relatively low-alcohol content beer is made from mashed-up maize or sorghum, malt, yeast and water. It is thick, heavy, creamy, and slightly sour. It was traditionally made by the African women and drunk almost immediately.

SA'S HOPS

Whilst hops are predominantly grown in the northern hemisphere, the South African hops industry is the only hops industry in the world to be successful at low latitudes. SA has cultivated highly successful strains which have changed the field.

CRAFT BEER

Craft beers have become increasingly popular in South Africa and there are microbreweries starting up across the country. They all have one thing in common – a desire to brew something different, be it a coffee stout or a buchu blonde, a Hop-lace IPA or just a lager more malty than most. Craven Craft Lager, a product of Stellenbrau, a Stellenbosch brewery, beat some 38 finalists from around the world to win the prize for best lager at the Global Craft Beer Award contest in Germany.

TAVERN OF THE SEAS

The first hop garden was planted in the Cape by Jan van Riebeeck in 1652 resulting in the Cape's first hops beer. Only a year or two later Jan van Riebeeck wrote in his diary: 'Today, praise the Lord, wine was made for the first time from Cape grapes.' Cape Town, as a replenishment station on the Dutch East India route, soon became known as 'The Tavern of the Seas.'

SAB

South African Breweries (SAB) is the second-largest brewer in the world. Their history can be traced back to Charles Glass who started the Castle Brewery in 1883. SAB's listing in 1897 was the first industrial share on the Johannesburg Stock Exchange. Today, the company has a presence in more than 80 countries and employs more than 70 000 people.

LIQUOR MARKET

MARKET VOLUME		MARKET VALUE
3.0 %	SPIRITS	21.1 %
8.5 %	WINE	11.5 %
9.9 %	READY TO DRINK	13.3 %
78.1 %	BEER	54.1 %

Source: Liquor Consumption Patterns in South Africa, Elias Holtzkampf 2013

THE WINE INDUSTRY

- There are over 100 000 hectares of vineyards in South Africa
- South Africa exports around 450 million litres of wine annually
- SA is the ninth-largest producer of wine in the world

WINE AWARDS

South African wines consistently win top accolades and trounce the competition annually in both the red and white single varietal categories at the prestigious international World Wine Awards.

PINOTAGE & CHENIN BLANC

Chenin Blanc is historically the most widely planted variety but more recently there is a notable shift from 80 % white grapes to a split that is nearly 50/50 red and white.

Pinotage is a uniquely South African grape variety. There are now plantings in other countries, but the origin of Pinotage is South African and it has achieved international success. Pinotage is especially well paired with venison and a South African braai.

FAIRTRADE

South Africa is recognised as the world leader in sustainable and ethical wine production and has won the prestigious Fairtrade Award. Of the 41 Fairtrade producers of wine, 20 of them are from South Africa.

SPOILT FOR CHOICE

Wine tasting steps to discover and explore the fruit of the vine from the hundreds of wine farms and estates:

- **READ AND ASK:** The back labels give clues about the wine's flavours, the ageing process, the region and even awards and reviews.
- **SWIRL:** Look for the slender lines of liquid that slowly drip down the sides of the glass. These give you a clue about the wine's alcohol content.
- **SNIFF:** Identify the smell. Honey? Peppers? Apple? Oak? The more you smell, the better the wine may taste.
- **SIP:** Let the liquid move around your tongue to pick up the many different flavours.
- **GOOD VINTAGE:** Do some research into the year and the regions. A perfectly ripe harvest - and good wines - are dependent on the climate and weather conditions.
- **DON'T BE FOOLED BY AGE:** 'Older wines aren't necessarily better'.

Wine

Apartheid Absurdity

Forgiven, not forgotten

Apartheid is behind us and the stories written into history, will never be repeated. Whilst we would like to forget this dark time in our past, it does remind us of just how far we have journeyed. In a book titled *Apartheid The Lighter Side* by Ben Maclennan, he recounts some newspaper articles of real-life situations from this tragic time.

THE MAIN APARTHEID LEGISLATION EXPLAINED:

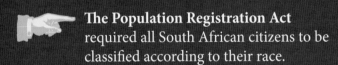 **The Population Registration Act** required all South African citizens to be classified according to their race.

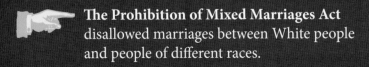 **The Prohibition of Mixed Marriages Act** disallowed marriages between White people and people of different races.

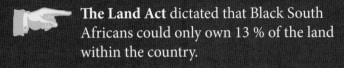 **The Land Act** dictated that Black South Africans could only own 13 % of the land within the country.

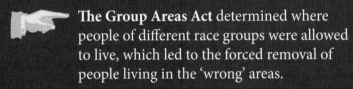 **The Group Areas Act** determined where people of different race groups were allowed to live, which led to the forced removal of people living in the 'wrong' areas.

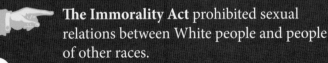 **The Immorality Act** prohibited sexual relations between White people and people of other races.

The Sunday Times
30 November, 1986

Three Johannesburg bus routes will be open to passengers of all races from tomorrow as a six-month experiment. Says Jan Van Blerk, vice-chairman of the city council's Transportation Committee, the experiment 'applies to Black buses as well as White. Fares are much lower on Black buses. So Blacks who want to travel on White buses will have to pay the higher fare while Whites will pay less if they travel on Black buses.' *A week later The Sunday Times attempted to clarify the situation by explaining to commuters that 'Blacks can ride on a White bus with a blue board on the front. Whites can only get on a Black bus with a yellow indicator board. What's more, 'blue' buses only stop at White bus stops. 'Yellow' buses only stop at Black stops.' A Whites-only bus stop was marked by a white sign with black type, and a white-on-black sign depicted a Blacks-only stop. And if you had to go to a public convenience while waiting for the right bus, you had to remember that a white figure on a green background meant a toilet was for Whites only; a green figure on white meant Black only.*

The Sunday Express
24 October, 1971

Coloured girls can now work as usherettes in White cinemas, provided they do not look at the screen, Mr John Redman, general manager of Ster Kinekor's theatre division, told me this week.

'When we show a film which our non-White girls are not allowed to see, they usher patrons with a torch and watch the floor,' he said.

We discussed the matter with the Department of Labour and I raised this point with them. As a precautionary measure, since non-Whites are not allowed to see some films restricted to Whites only, we decided that they should not look at the screen.'

The Cape Times
21 October, 1960

The police report to the Paarl Liquor Licensing Board issued yesterday emphasises that, in all cases, glasses for Whites and non-Whites are to be washed separately and kept apart. Separate cloths must also be used for drying the glasses and kept apart.

The Cape Times
27 January, 1990

A City surgeon yesterday criticised as 'disgraceful' a refusal by the Volkshospitaal in Gardens to admit a Black domestic worker who needed urgent surgery. He said there was no place in medicine for racial discrimination. However, Dr John Moodie, regional director of Medical Services, said the patient was not turned away because of the colour of her skin but because the three beds reserved for Blacks at the hospital were full.

The Business Day
29 September, 1988

'A White Bronkhorstspruit family said yesterday funeral plans for a relative had to be changed when their church refused to allow a Black maid to attend the ceremony. The Nederduitsch Hervormde Kerk in Bronkhorstspruit refused to allow Sarah Mashiani to attend Tuesday's funeral of her employer, Lita Venter, 71. 'According to church law the church is for Whites only,' a spokesman said. The service was moved to the town's more progressive Nederduitse Gereformeerde Kerk.'

The Cape Times
2 March, 1961

The group areas act defined three races, Dr van Rensburg said – 'White, Native and Coloured'. All those who fell between the White and Native were regarded as Coloured. But the Act allowed the Coloured group to be subdivided into Indian, Chinese, Malays and those commonly known as Coloured people. The Malays were regarded as Malays only as long as they lived in their own group area of Schotsche Kloof. If they moved into another area, even across the road, they became Coloureds. A Japanese, as far as the Act was concerned, was 'Coloured' because, by definition, he did not fall into any other group.

The Act did not have a definition of a Japansese. But a Japanese living in the Union could get permission to live as a White, buy houses in White areas, and attend White cinemas and restaurants. But any Japanese tourist would technically be Coloured. However, he could once again be treated as a White and book in at the best hotels for a maximum period of 90 days. - Dr Van Rensburg was chairman of the Group Areas Board.

The Cape Times
24 September, 1966

'In my opinion the kissing of a non-White girl in a dark secluded spot in a car is against public morals and constitutes an offence under the Immorality Act' - Boksburg magistrate, Mr G Smit, convicting a 25-year-old White man under the Immorality Act for kissing an African woman. Sentence: one month in gaol, suspended for a year.

The Cape Times
18 December, 1964

Two Chinese women are being bleached white at the Sterkfontein Mental Institution, near Krugerdorp, to prepare them for transfer from non-White wards to the White section. A special bleaching lotion is applied to their faces and arms. For the first time in years they are being allowed to grow their hair long and visit the institution's beauty parlour, to re-accustom them to the European way of life. A hospital spokesman said: 'The women have been accommodated with Africans for years. Chinese are now entitled to treatment in White wards, but before we can move the women we must prepare them for the tremendous change. By bleaching their skins we are starting their rehabilitation. Not only will it be a psychological booster to them, but it will make them more acceptable to the White patients.'

South Africa is a land of contrast in so many ways. This is seen in the dramatic countryside, the diversity of the people and the discrepancies between the first- and third-world economy. There is nothing more contrasting, however, than the creatures with their camouflage and their brightness and beauty.

CAN YOU FIND US?

LIZARD, LEOPARD, NIGHTJAR, KLIPSPRINGER, ADDER AND ...BOTH THE CROCS!

Photos: Lizard, Maureen Pierre; Nightjar, Steve Coetzee; Frog, Marna Cilliers, Green Vision Foundation; Lizard, Debbie Patching-Bozza; Croc shoe, source: Facebook, origin unknown

South Africa - A land of
CONTRAST

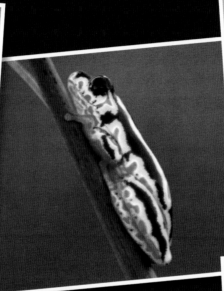

YOU CAN'T MISS US!

LOCUST, FROG, LIZARD, BUTTERFLY, KINGFISHER AND STRELITZIA.

1963
6.05
children

BIRTH RATE

Between 1963 and 2013 the average number of babies a South African woman gave birth to decreased significantly

1983
4.50
children

2013
2.38
children

IN 1904

the population was
5.1 MILLION PEOPLE

IN 1980

the population grew to
20.55 MILLION PEOPLE

IN 2011

the population reached
51.77 MILLION PEOPLE

The population doubled in the **30 years** between 1960 and 1991

The population is expected to take about **60 years** to double again!

PRESERVING OUR HERITAGE

OLDEST GAME RESERVE IN AFRICA

The Hluhluwe-iMfolozi Park in KwaZulu-Natal was proclaimed in 1895. The reserve is not only the oldest game park in Africa but also the second oldest in the world after the Yellow Stone of America.

• • •

BIGGEST GAME RESERVE IN SOUTH AFRICA

The Kruger National Park is 19 485 km² in area, almost the same size as the country of Israel.

• • •

FIRST OFFICIAL PROTECTED AREAS IN SOUTH AFRICA

The Knysna and Tsitsikamma Forest Reserves were proclaimed in terms of the Cape Forest Act of 1888.

• • •

OLDEST PRIVATELY OWNED RESERVE IN SOUTH AFRICA

The Sabi Sands Reserve is the birthplace of sustainable wildlife tourism in Southern Africa, and is the oldest private reserve in South Africa. The reserve has only ever been a wilderness area.

• • •

MOST SUCCESSFUL PRIVATE CONSERVATION INITIATIVE

Under the leadership of conservationist, Dr John O'Brien, **Shamwari Game Reserve** has been named the 'World's Leading Conservation Company' for 15 consecutive years at the annual World Travel Awards.

SOUTH AFRICA IS THE THIRD-MOST BIOLOGICALLY DIVERSE COUNTRY IN THE WORLD, AFTER INDONESIA AND BRAZIL.

Biodiversity means the number and variety of living organisms on earth. These three countries collectively contain more than two thirds of the global biodiversity and harbour most of the Earth's species.

There are over 100 000 known species of plants, animals and fungi in South Africa. Scientists believe that there are at least another 50 000 species in the country that have not yet been discovered and/or named.

There is evidence to suggest that elaborate natural resource management systems were applied by indigenous African people such as the San, Khoi and Nguni prior to the country's colonisation. King Shaka used the area of the current day iMfolozi Reserve as an exclusive royal hunting ground. History tells us that he implemented conservation laws in the region.

'Each one of us is intimately attached to the soil of this beautiful country. Each time one of us touches the soil of this land, we feel a sense of personal renewal.'

- Nelson Mandela, Inauguration Speech, 1994

'Black or White, the footprints
left in the dirt are the same.'

- Sam Clark

Heritage Day

Heritage Day was originally known as Shaka Day. The day was a commemoration by the KwaZulu-Natal Zulus of the death of their Zulu King, Shaka. In 1994 parliament rejected Shaka Day as a public holiday and the Inkatha Freedom Party, a party with a large Zulu membership, objected. A compromise was eventually reached by changing the essence of Heritage Day to reflect the identity of *all* South Africans.

Heritage Day is now a day on which all genders, races and cultural groups commemorate their histories. It is a day for remembering the contributions many individuals have made to their heritage. And it is a day when South Africans acknowledge their *diversity within unity*. Visiting heritage sites on Heritage Day as a way of celebrating the diversity of South African culture has become a popular pastime.

Definition of Heritage: the features belonging to the culture of a particular society, such as traditions, languages, or buildings, that were created in the past and still have historical importance today.

i am an African!

Thabo Mbeki gave a moving and eloquent speech at the adoption of the Constitutional Bill in 1996. His words convey how our identity as Africans is drawn from the indelible beauty of our land and its ancestors. They leave us with a deep sense of humility, wonder and gratitude.

I owe my being to the hills and the valleys, the mountains and the glades, the rivers, the deserts, the trees, the flowers, the seas and the ever-changing seasons that define the face of our native land.

My body has frozen in our frosts and in our latter-day snows. It has thawed in the warmth of our sunshine and melted in the heat of the midday sun. The crack and the rumble of the summer thunders, lashed by startling lightning, have been a cause both of trembling and of hope.

The fragrances of nature have been as pleasant to us as the sight of the wild blooms of the citizens of the veld.

The dramatic shapes of the Drakensberg, the soil-coloured waters of the Lekoa, iGqili noThukela, and the sands of the Kgalagadi, have all been panels of the set on the natural stage on which we act out the foolish deeds of the theatre of our day.

At times, and in fear, I have wondered whether I should concede equal citizenship of our country to the leopard and the lion, the elephant and the springbok, the hyena, the black mamba and the pestilential mosquito.

A human presence among all these, a feature on the face of our native land thus defined, I know that none dare challenge me when I say - I am an African!

I owe my being to the Khoi and the San whose desolate souls haunt the great expanses of the beautiful Cape - they who fell victim to the most merciless genocide our native land has ever seen, they who were the first to lose their lives in the struggle to defend our freedom and independence and they who, as a people, perished as a result.

Today, as a country, we keep an audible silence about these ancestors of the generations that live, fearful to admit the horror of a former deed, seeking to obliterate from our memories a cruel occurrence which, in its remembering, should teach us not and never to be inhuman again.

I am formed of the migrants who left Europe to find a new home on our native land. Whatever their own actions, they remain still part of me.

In my veins courses the blood of the Malay slaves who came from the East. Their proud dignity informs my bearing, their culture a part of my essence. The stripes they bore on their bodies from the lash of the slave master are a reminder embossed on my consciousness of what should not be done.

I am the grandchild of the warrior men and women that Hintsa and Sekhukhune led, the patriots that Cetshwayo and Mphephu took to battle, the soldiers Moshoeshoe and Ngungunyane taught never to dishonour the cause of freedom.

Being part of all these people, and in the knowledge that none dare contest that assertion, I shall claim that - I am an African!

Today it feels good to be an African!

Largest green canyon
in the world

The Blyde River Canyon (recently re-named the Motlatse Canyon Provincial Nature Reserve) is said to be the third deepest canyon in the world (after the Grand Canyon in the US and the Fish River Canyon in Namibia) and the **largest 'green canyon' due to its lush, subtropical foliage**. The spectacular cliffs, situated below the confluence of the *Blyde* ('joy') and *Treur* ('sorrow') rivers, rise between 600 m and 800 m from the river bed and extend over 20 km in length.

Blyde (Motlatse) River Canyon, Mpumalanga

SHOPPING

DESPITE THE FIRST-WORLD OPTIONS, THE 'ONLY IN AFRICA' REMINDERS WILL ALWAYS MAKE SHOPPING AN INTERESTING PASTIME.

When it comes to shopping, South Africans are spoilt for choice. World-class shopping centres offer chain stores, speciality stores and boutiques together with entertainment, movies and delicious food options.

Canal Walk in Cape Town is the largest shopping centre in Africa in a lettable area, however, the mammoth Gateway Theatre of Shopping in Durban is larger in total area, and if you include the Nelson Mandela Square annex, then the Sandton City complex in Johannesburg is the largest. They are the biggest shopping centres in Africa and arguably, in the southern hemisphere.

TAKE AWAY
AFRICAN SPICE
RUSSIAN & CHIPS
CHICKEN & CHIPS
FISH & CHIPS
FAT COCK
COFFEE & TEA
CORN FLAKES
CIGARETTES
TURKEY
AIR TIME

Home deliveries via trolley give shopping a whole new meaning!

TEETH ARE CLEAN TRY THEM ON!

Don't forget to stop for coffee and, South Africa's favourite, vetkoek - pronounced 'fet-cook'.

Special deliveries made to Dempsey's Guest House!

Who says shopping is boring when you can order '**germ free**' gem squash, self-basting turkeys that are '**self-bursting**' and '**sting rolls**' that look like spring rolls. Don't forget to come home with the low fat spread that '**farts**' and beef mince made from '**bees**'. In the absence of tongs, please don't forget to use your **tongue** to pick up the bread rolls!

Get smart today   smart shopper

PNP
SELF BURSTING
TURKEY

29⁹⁹ P/KG

GREAT SAVI

GERMS SQUASH PK 4.99 100G

SOFT
SERVE ASS

FLAVOUR

2⁵⁰ EACH

DO NOT TOUCH BREAD WITH HANDS
PLEASE USE TONGUE

OLE
LOW FART SPREAD 5⁹⁹ 500G   8⁹⁹

www.engrish.com

STING ROLLS VEGETABLE 6⁹⁹ / EACH

SPECIAL

BEE MINCE 80/20
R 49.98.98 P/KG

SPECIAL   SPECIAL

Best Wishes Suzanne
Under Neat that
We will Miss you

A customer got quite a surprise when she collected her specially iced cake for a going-away party. Her order which she gave telephonically was to be '**Best Wishes Suzanne**' and underneath that '**We will miss you**'.

THE BIGGEST BOX OFFICE HIT EVER

DISNEY'S LION KING

showcases the best of what Africa has to offer from beautiful plains to the majestic wildlife. The story brings to life the reality of the delicate balance of our existence and interaction with one another.

THE SOUTH AFRICAN BEHIND THE STORY

Lebohang 'Lebo M' Morake is the renowned composer behind much of the film's music. Born in Soweto in 1964, he left school at age nine to become a performer. Whilst in exile in Lesotho, a US ambassador recognised his talent and arranged for him to attend the Duke Ellington School of Music in Washington. His iconic voice, which is heard in the opening scene's chant, 'Nants Ingonyama' has become synonymous with *The Lion King*.

THE LION SLEEPS

The original song titled *In the Jungle* was written in 1939 by Solomon Linda from Zululand who signed over the copyright for next to nothing. It is said the original song was probably the first African record to sell 100 000 copies. The song achieved worldwide fame. A South African author and songwriter documented the inequity of the situation in the Rolling Stones magazine. Thereafter, although Disney had used the song in good faith, a lawsuit ensued over the royalties of the song. The matter was subsequently settled to everyone's satisfaction.

THE CIRCLE OF LIFE

Elton John's memorable track is so much more than just a song; the song 'Circle of Life' as depicted in the story highlights that no one is immortal and that one's time on earth is a precious gift not to be abused. The importance of the 'circle of life' is that all living things must walk it together in balanced harmony. This song presents the thought philosophy that if something dies, it gives new life to another.

Mufasa: *Everything you see exists together in a delicate balance. As king, you need to understand that balance and respect all the creatures, from the crawling ant to the leaping antelope.*

Simba: *But, Dad, don't we eat the antelope?*

Mufasa: *Yes, Simba, but let me explain. When we die, our bodies become the grass, and the antelope eat the grass. And so we are all connected in the great **Circle of Life**.*

THE LION

WORLDWIDE SUCCESS

September 2014 saw *The Lion King* become the top-earning title in box-office history with a worldwide gross of $6.2 billion displacing Andrew Lloyd Webber's *The Phantom of the Opera*. This record is for both stage productions and films. Cumulative Worldwide Box Office places *The Lion King* way ahead of top-grossing film, *Avatar*, as well as *Titanic* and the individual *Star Wars* or *Harry Potter* titles.

LION STATS

- In the wild, lions rest for around 20 hours a day.
- The roar of a lion can be heard from 8 km away
- A litter of lion cubs contains three to four cubs
- Africa has lost up to 80 % - 90 % of the lion population since 1975. It now stands at about 21 000.
- Their top speed is 81 km/h over short distances.
- The average male's weight is between 150 kg and 227 kg.

KING

LESSONS FROM THE LION KING

HAKUNA MATATA

This is one of the most memorable lessons to take away from the movie. 'Hakuna Matata' is Swahili for 'there are no worries' and, in short, teaches us not to sweat the small stuff. We only live once and need to make the most of every day!

LEARN FROM THE PAST

Just as Simba discovers that he is unable to escape the effects of his father's death, we learn that the past will always be a part of us and makes us who we are. Although we cannot run from the past, we can learn from it and allow it to help us move forward.

WE CAN ACCOMPLISH GREAT THINGS

All we need is to realise that anything is possible. Although Simba doubted himself, with the help of Rafiki, he was able to defeat his uncle Scar, rise to greatness and achieve his true potential.

UNLIKELY ACQUAINTANCES MAKE THE GREATEST FRIENDS

Timone and Pumba are unlikely friends - physically they could not be more different. But this meerkat and warthog become the best of friends proving that it is what is on the inside that counts and that the greatest friendships come in the most unexpected forms.

TREAT OTHERS AS YOU WISH TO BE TREATED

No matter what a person's position or accomplishments, each person is significant and adds value to the world in unique ways. Mufasa explains that even though the lion is 'king of the jungle' and on top of the food chain, every animal must be respected for their own dignity and contribution.

Legendary Journeys

The International Traveller
Passage to Rebellion

In 1613, a Khoikhoi chief named Xhore (Coree), became the first ever, albeit unwilling, African to voyage to England. The Dutch East India Company and the British East India Company had both set their sights on the strategically situated Cape of Good Hope. As part of their efforts at establishing a settlement there, a British ship, the *Hector*, called in at Table Bay. Coree boarded the ship to trade with the captain when suddenly the ship hauled anchor and sailed away with the 'kidnapped' Coree. The plan was to take Coree to England where he was to undergo 'training' in the English language, clothing and culture. It was intended that the 'Anglicised' Coree would then return to the Cape and assist the British in their colonisation and expansion plans. Although Coree was treated like visiting royalty, their plan backfired. Coree flatly rejected the teaching and asked to be sent home. Upon his return to South Africa, instead of furthering the European agenda, he told his people not to trust the British. Coree was eventually killed in 1626 by a Dutch trader. His mistrust of the White man was inherited by his sons who were instrumental in the first Khoikhoi-Dutch war of 1658.

Portuguese Explorers
Voyage of the Unknown

In 1488 the Portuguese explorer Bartolomeu Dias was the first European seafarer to sail round the Cape. This opened the way for the discovery of a sea route around Africa to India.

Nine years later his fellow countryman, Vasco da Gama, was assigned to push on to India. Aboard the *Sao Gabriel* with 148 men as crew, Da Gama and his men ransacked the Arabian ships on the coast of East Africa, making a few enemies along the way. Although he lost half his crew to scurvy on that voyage, the trip was not in vain. Da Gama became the first European explorer to find the sea route to India, which in turn helped develop the spice trade. South Africa became the halfway stopping point, a fact which also led to the colonisation of Mozambique by the Portuguese.

These Portuguese explorer discoveries made for improved trade overall and established South Africa's place in the realm of trading. Ironically, Dias died in 1500, lost at sea near the cape which he had named the Cape of Storms.

> *Tales of epic journeys fill South Africa's history books, immortalising the events and the people in the process. Different cultural groups, for various reasons, have embarked on pioneering journeys, encountering violent conflict, disease, hope and despair along the way.*

Mandela Release
Journey to Freedom

In the culmination of a journey of many decades, on 11 February 1990 Nelson Mandela stepped onto the balcony of Cape Town's City Hall to address a nation of joyous supporters.

He expressed his humble and heartfelt gratitude to 'millions of my compatriots and those in every corner of the globe who have campaigned tirelessly for my release.' In happy celebration of this historical occasion, South Africans across the nation danced ecstatically in the streets.

Mandela's trip from the Victor Verster prison just outside Paarl to the balcony in Cape Town was a relatively short one. However, the trip was symbolic of a life-long journey which started long before his 27-year imprisonment. Following Tata Madiba's release from prison, South Africa saw the apartheid laws relaxing. Mandela's release became a symbol for the birth of a new South Africa and was a catalyst for the democracy that is celebrated today.

Great Trek
Pilgrimage for Independence

The Great Trek began in 1835 when, over a period of three years, more than 12 000 Boers (farmers) left the Cape Colony in search of farmland and an independent livelihood. One of their leaders, Piet Retief, described their mission as a journey 'to govern ourselves without interference'.

Often described as the bravest of travellers, the Voortrekkers (pioneer trekkers) moved in groups on horseback and by ox-wagon, making their way inland and then to the north and east. Their journey was fraught with difficulty and danger. Conflict with the indigenous inhabitants, disputes amongst themselves, harsh weather and illness beset them as they travelled vast distances over rough terrain. Those who crossed the Drakensberg into Natal fought against the Zulu people, and the republic that they founded was soon annexed by the British. Many trekked away again to join the groups that settled down to farm in the interior. There they saw their dreams of self-government and independence come true as they established the republics of the Orange Free State and the Transvaal.

Their freedom did not last, however. The discovery of diamonds and gold in these territories promised wealth but created new tensions between the Boers and the British. After the British victory in the second Anglo-Boer War (to the Boers, it was a 'Vryheidsoorlog', or war for freedom) the trekker republics were annexed to Britain and then, in 1910, incorporated into the Union of South Africa as part of the British Empire.

Although the dream of a fully independent South African republic would not be realised until 1961, the Great Trek contributed to the development of the Afrikaans language and the establishment of a farming community with a strong sense of identity. The pioneering journey of the Voortrekkers and the history of the Afrikaners are commemorated in the majestic Voortrekker Monument near Pretoria (Tshwane).

BEFORE

AFTER

Photo courtesy of www.active-escapes.co.za

Photos courtesy of Facebook - Africa, this is why I live here

Doug Molton
Lions River
June 2012

152

CYCLING AFRICAN STYLE!

DID YOU KNOW?

→ The eight-day stage race, the Absa Cape Epic, is the **most televised** mountain bike race in the world.

→ The Cape Cycle Tour is the **largest, timed cycling event** in the world with 35 000 cyclists participating.

→ The Nedbank Sani2c is the **world's biggest mountain biking** stage race.

→ South African Mountain Biker, Greg Minnaar, holds three **Downhill World Champion titles** and is three times the Downhill World Cup Champion; he has achieved 18 Downhill World Cup victories.

→ South Africa is said to have the **highest per capita spending** on cycling equipment in the world.

→ Cycling is arguably the **fastest-growing sport** in South Africa, poised to usurp the prized position long held by golf as the corporate sport of choice.

→ Pietermaritzburg has hosted the **UCI Mountain Bike World Cup** for six of the eight years since 2009.

0:07 / 1:15

Mountain Biker gets taken out by BUCK - Only in Africa
Check it out on www.youtube.com   **15, 341, 641** views

POPULATION DESTROYERS

THROUGH THE YEARS EVENTS OF SUCH MAGNITUDE HAVE OCCURRED THAT THEY SIGNIFICANTLY, AND IN MANY INCIDENCES, PERMANENTLY CHANGED THE POPULATION OF THE COUNTRY.

DIRTY LAUNDRY

THE SMALLPOX EPIDEMIC WIPES OUT 90 % OF THE KHOIKHOI POPULATION

When a Dutch ship arrived at the Cape in 1713 to top up their food supplies the crew were infected with the deadly smallpox disease. They sent their clothing and linen to the slave lodge for cleaning and in so doing contaminated the colonist population. The disease soon reached pandemic proportions. It was foreign to the indigenous Khoikhoi people whose traditional medicines were ineffective. The Khoi were fearful of the colonists and the 'evil death' which they brought so they fled - only to be killed by unaffected Khoi groups whom they encountered.

By the end of the year, whole clans of Khoikhoi were annihilated and not even 10 % of the original Khoi population of the southwestern Cape had survived the epidemic. The few Khoi survivors without their clans lost their indigenous clan names. And it was at this point in history that the Khoikhoi became known by the derogatory term 'Hottentots'.

BOGUS PROPHECY

OVER 40 000 XHOSA PEOPLE STARVE TO DEATH

A 14-year-old girl named Nongqawuse was believed to be a prophetess. The year was 1856 and the Xhosa people would do anything to drive the Europeans from their lands. The girl told the Xhosa people that the spirits had advised them to destroy all their crops and kill their cattle. This would result in the European settlers being driven into the sea. In return the Xhosa people's cattle and crops would be replaced by an even better yield. Believing these words to be from the spirits, the entire nation heeded her advice and destroyed over 400 000 cattle and all of their crops.

The result was that within a year the number of Xhosa people dropped from 105 000 to less than 27 000 people. Those that did not starve to death migrated to other areas and some even resorted to cannibalism. Without the protection of their tribe, the Xhosa who survived found themselves as servants of the British.

YEAR OF DEATH

THE CATTLE PLAGUE KILLS OVER 2.5 MILLION CATTLE

The rinderpest epidemic in the 1890s decimated almost 90 % of all sub-Saharan cattle as well as significant numbers of eland, buffalo, wildebeest, giraffe and antelope. In South Africa the resulting loss of over 2.5 million cattle caused widespread poverty and famine in what was later referred to as 'The year of the rinderpest'. Rinderpest, or cattle plague, travelled down Africa and first appeared in South Africa in 1896. Attempts to contain the spread with a barbed-wire fence about a thousand miles long just south of the *Orange River* were unsuccessful. Police patrols were set up and European travellers from the north were admitted only after disinfection of their clothes. The entrance of Africans was practically prohibited.

Immunisation research undertaken in Kimberley resulted in a successful solution and before the end of 1898 more than two million head of cattle had been inoculated. At the end of 1898 rinderpest was under control and temporarily disappeared from South Africa.

154

BLOOD SUCKERS

MALARIA EPIDEMICS CAUSE THE DEATH OF THOUSANDS

Malaria was initially thought to come from marshes and swamps hence the name mal-aria (bad air). It was only in the 1890s that the cause was attributed to a parasite transmitted by the female anopheline mosquitoes. One of the first well-documented cases of the devastating effects of malaria in South Africa was probably that of Louis Trichardt. He, together with 20 of his 53 members of his party, died on their trek to Mozambique in 1837-38. The great explorer David Livingstone also succumbed to the disease. Disease outbreaks also occurred in Natal (first in 1905) and Zululand. Epidemics caused the deaths of over 20 000 people in a single season and the disease spread as far south as Port St Johns. Severe malaria epidemics occurred in Natal from 1929 to 1933. During this time railway construction and sugar production came to a standstill and almost one million quinine tablets were distributed by the health authorities. The disease also spread to the former Transvaal where almost 10 000 deaths were reported in the 1930s.

The breakthrough came with the availability and use of DDT and other long-lasting insecticides. Although their use was highly controversial their application resulted in a dramatic interruption of malaria transmission in virtually all areas. Nowadays, although the disease is currently responsible for killing over 600 000 people a year around the world, of which 92 % are in sub-Saharan Africa, the disease is under control in South Africa and confined to the very narrow band in the low-lying areas on the northeastern borders of the country with as few as 70 deaths annually.

SHIPS OF DEATH

RETURNING SOLDIERS BRING DEATHLY DISEASE

Called the 'Spanish Flu', the influenza epidemic that broke out in 1918 led to the deaths of 50 million people worldwide. It reached South Africa in September 1918 and within six weeks around 300 000 South Africans had died of the disease.

The First World War, while not the direct cause of its outbreak, contributed to its rapid spread worldwide. It is thought that the ships of soldiers returning from the war docked at Sierra Leone, one of the places regarded as a central point of infection. A number of factors contributed to the rapid spread of the epidemic throughout South Africa. South Africa had a number of ports and harbours from which sailors and soldiers spread the infection. By 1918 the country had a well-developed railway network of 16 000 km making it easier for the epidemic to penetrate the most remote areas. The migrant labour system ensured that the virus travelled with infected miners on their way to the mines or homes.

In total, about half a million people are believed to have died of the epidemic in South Africa, making it the fifth hardest-hit country in the world.

POLITICAL HOGWASH

OVER 300 000 DEATHS ATTRIBUTED TO GOVERNMENT'S POLICY ON HIV

Former Minister of Health, Mantombazana Tshabala-Msimang, became known as 'Dr Beetroot' because of her claim that HIV does not cause AIDS and that eating vegetables, beetroot, garlic and other nutritional foods was a cure for the deadly virus.

Nine years were wasted while the AIDS pandemic raged on. The government maintained a belief that if the problem of Black poverty as a whole was addressed then the issue of HIV and AIDS would no longer be a problem. A battle began for the provision of anti-retroviral drugs (ARVs) but the government resisted. Finally, increased pressure from civil society resulted in the South African cabinet approving a plan for universal ARV treatment but the programme was slow to get started and by late 2005 more than five million South Africans were HIV-positive, making South Africa the country with the highest HIV infection rate in the world.

Since the public sector made widespread ARV treatment available it has made strides in altering perspectives of HIV/AIDS among South Africans. A diagnosis of HIV, which was understood by many as a death sentence, has increasingly been seen as treatable and manageable.

The impact of the government HIV policy can be seen in the life expectancy statistics of the country. In 1993 the average life expectancy was 62 years. It dropped down to 53 years in 2003 and then after the ARV programme was finally implemented it rose to 57 years in 2013.

Photo © Stuart Taylor

LIVING ON AFRICAN TIME!

NOW ...NOW NOW ...JUST NOW ...LATER
...WHENEVER!

Oxford Dictionary Definition:

Now now: *adverb* (South African informal)
Used to refer to a time very shortly before or very soon after the moment of speaking.

THE SPECTACLE OF THREE MILLION BARN SWALLOWS

The Barn Swallows at Mount Moreland Inkonjane provide a spectacular display of as many as three million birds circling and descending to roost each evening. October heralds the Barn Swallows' arrival from the North and millions of these amazing migrants begin to appear over the Mount Moreland Inkonjane roosting site. The swallows roost in the wetlands which flank this coastal village of Northern KwaZulu-Natal. Early in March the swallows become far more vocal and start preparing for the forthcoming breeding season, flying in pairs in an almost flirtatious pattern with their new coat of feathers. By mid-April the Barn Swallows have departed on their long journey of up to 12 000 km to their European destinations, flying a distance of about 400 km in a single day.

The Barn Swallow site is listed as a global Important Bird Area (IBA). Mount Moreland qualifies as an IBA because it houses more than 1 % of the global population of Barn Swallows. The global number of Barn Swallows is estimated at 190 million mature individuals, and Mount Moreland has well over three million individuals. Although not an endangered species, the swallows receive much attention because they are one of the world's smallest migratory birds with a lifestyle which often brings them into close proximity with humans. The swallows provide an invaluable indicator of the health of the local environment.

King Shaka International Airport was built very near the site of the Barn Swallows' nesting site. Bird radar and a Swallow Detection Algorithm are used to track the movements of the swallow flocks in the early mornings and late afternoons. Data collected since 2007 indicate that the airport and the swallows can easily co-exist. This is the first commercial airport where information from a bird detection radar is used actively by air traffic controllers to warn pilots of current bird strike risks.

158

Photo courtesty of Angie Wilken

SOUTH AFRICA'S
COAT OF ARMS

A national coat of arms, or State emblem, is the highest visual symbol of the State. Important documents in your life, for example birth and marriage certificates and passports, are endorsed by the Coat of Arms. Coins have the Coat of Arms on one side.

!KE E: /XARRA //KE

ELEPHANT TUSKS

The tusks of the African elephant, reproduced in pairs to represent men and women, symbolise wisdom, steadfastness and strength.

TWO FIGURES

The two figures greeting each other symbolise unity.

SPEAR & KNOBKERRIE

Symbolise authority and defence. They are shown lying down to depict peace. They also represent the Secretary bird's legs.

PROTECTIVE SHIELD

The shield shows both identity and spiritual defence.

!KE E: /XARRA //KE

UNITY IN DIVERSITY

The motto derives from the Khoisan language of the /Xam people. This language is now extinct. By inscribing the words 'Unity in Diversity' on our Coat of Arms we acknowledge the tragedy of human beings who have perished because of people's inhumanity to others. Consequently we make a commitment to value life, to respect all languages and cultures and to oppose racism, sexism, chauvinism and genocide.

It is not our diversity which divides us; it is not our ethnicity or religion or culture that divides us. Since we have achieved our freedom, there can only be one division amongst us: between those who cherish democracy and those who do not.'

- Nelson Mandela

PROTEA FLOWER

An emblem of the beauty of the land, it symbolises the flowering of the nation.

SECRETARY BIRD

The bird is a symbol of protection and a messenger bringing grace to the earth. The uplifted wings refer to the ascendance of the nation.

RISING SUN

A symbol of the rebirth and the source of life, light and the wholeness of humanity.

EARS OF WHEAT

As the emblem of fertility, they symbolise growth and development.

BRAAI

INVENTED BY
CAVEMEN
PERFECTED BY
SOUTH AFRICANS

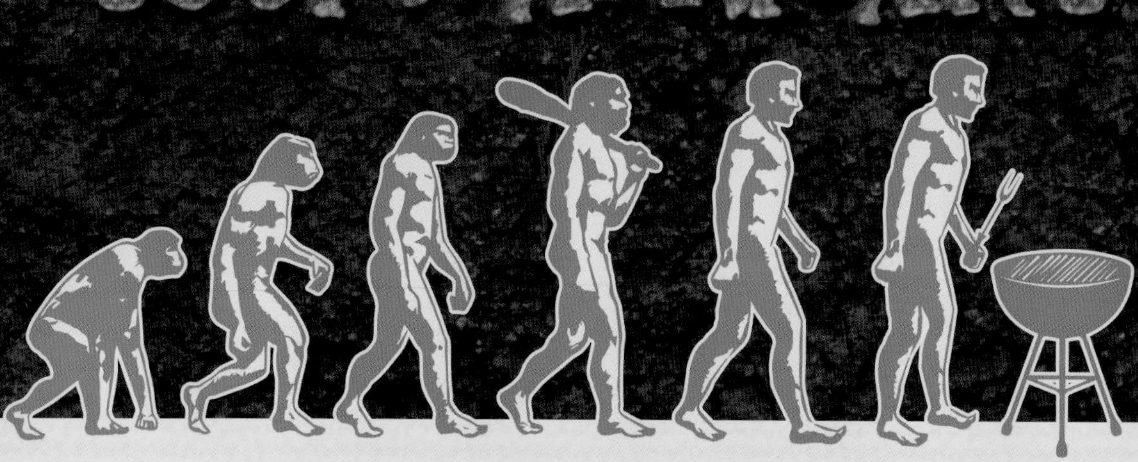

As South Africans, braaing is a part of us – it is in our blood – it is our heritage - our culture - our way of life. In fact many would say it's the reason for living!

Cooking meat outdoors, over an open fire, was a simple necessity in the early days of colonial settlement but was popularised during the Great Trek centenary celebrations in 1938.

A bring and braai means friends and family arrive with sosaties, boerewors, chops, ribbetjies, steaks and Nik Naks in hand and ... Let's not forget the dop! Dop is the South African word for alcohol, something that flows at these gatherings. You will often hear braai participants speak of bringing their klippies and coke, spook and diesel or even a generous stash of local beers. This being said, it is no surprise that the average braai is called a 'bokdopentjop', in other words bring your woman (bok), your drinks (dop) and your meat (tjop)!

South Africans are strange people. When we feel down, we braai. When we want to celebrate, we braai. When we are bored, we braai. When we have something to talk about, we braai. When we have nothing to talk about, we braai. So bring your meat,

LET'S BRAAI!

Kulula's 2014 annual April Fool's joke (at least we think it's one!) was to offer passengers an option of a chop 'braaied in the sky' when booking their tickets online. It was not too clear where in the aeroplane the meat would be braaied!

THE BOKSBURG THESAURUS OF COMPUTER TERMINOLOGY

LOG ON Make the braai hotter

LOG OFF The braai is too hot

DOWNLOAD Get the firewood off the bakkie

HARD DRIVE Trip back home without any cold beer

MONITOR Keeping an eye on the braai

BYTE What mosquitoes do – before the braai

MEGA BYTE What mosquitoes do – after a few beers

SOFTWARE Plastic knives and forks (from KFC)

HARDWARE Stainless steel knives and forks (from Checkers)

USER The dude who keeps taking the braai tongs

CURSOR The bloke around the braai who swears a lot

YAHOO What you say when the braai meat is ready to go

TOP 10 BRAAI MOVIE TITLES

Braai Hard
Braai the Beloved Country
Braai Another Day
Live and Let Braai
Four Weddings and a Braai
Close encounters of the third braai
Braai-Trek
Braai on Elm Street
Braai Freedom
Not Another Braai Movie

know you're South African when… you have a braai not a BBQ because BBQ is a chip flavour!

Rhino Poaching

Rhino horn is estimated to be worth over R 700 000 (US $ 60 000) per kilogram on the black market, making it worth more than gold, platinum, diamonds and even cocaine - a dramatic increase since 2006 when the value was just over R 9000 ($ 760).

The current poaching crisis is attributed to the growing demand for rhino horn in Asian countries, mainly Vietnam and China. Vietnam has been identified as the largest user of rhino horn. According to the people who sell it in the markets of East Asia, powdered rhino horn can serve as everything from a cure for cancer to an all-purpose health tonic, a sexual stimulant, a hangover cure and a treatment for high fever. Studies prove that you would be better off with an aspirin or biting your nails.

Rhinos were once abundant throughout Africa and Asia with an approximated worldwide population of 500 000 in the early 20th century. The western black rhino was declared extinct by the IUCN (International Union for Conservation of Nature) in 2011, with the primary cause identified as poaching. However, all five remaining rhinos species are listed on the IUCN Red List of Threatened Species, with three out of five species classified as critically endangered. South Africa is home to 82 % of Africa's rhino in total, including 93 % of the continent's white rhinos and 39 % of its black rhinos.

**RHINO HORN
DOES NOT
MAKE YOU LOOK YOUNGER
MAKE YOU MORE FERTILE
FREE YOU FROM DEMONS
CURE TYPHOID OR FLU
IT JUST
KILLS RHINOS!**

Rhino Witness Protection programme

Rhinos are currently being released onto undisclosed (and secret) locations in South Africa. The animals form part of the WWF South Africa's Black Rhino Range Expansion Project (BRREP). Black rhino are more at risk of extinction than white rhino due to their low numbers. Since the start of the programme in 2003, BRREP has overseen the relocation of around 160 black rhino to form new breeding populations and more than 50 calves have been born on project sites.

"Let us not look back in anger, but forward in fury.

— Dr. Ian Player

4800
Black rhino in Africa

20 000
White rhino in Africa

Black rhino VS White rhino

Black rhino are actually grey.

They are browsers and use their pointed upper lips to twist off the low-growing branches of trees and shrubs.

They eat woody trees, shrubs and herbs.

Black rhino grow to 1.6 m tall and weigh up to 1400 kg.

Black rhino run at a top speed of 55 km per hour.

White rhino are also grey.

The name 'white' rhino is said to come from the Dutch word 'wijd' as in 'wide-mouthed' rhino.

They are grazers and eat mainly grasses.

White rhino grow to 1.8 m and weigh over two tons.

White rhino run at a speed of 40-50 km per hour.

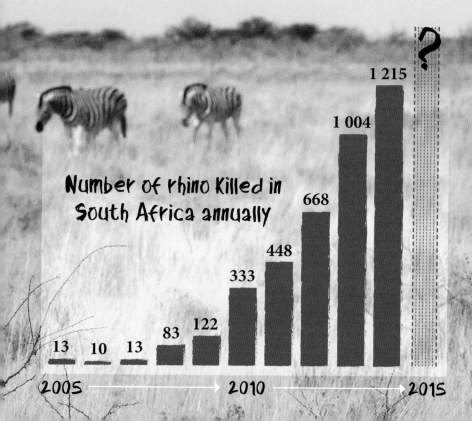

Number of rhino killed in South Africa annually

13   10   13   83   122   333   448   668   1 004   1 215   ?

2005   2010   2015

Only when the last of the animals' horns, tusks, skin and bones are sold, will mankind realise that money can never buy back our wildlife.

World's largest natural fountain: Kuruman (20 million litres of water daily)

Largest underwater cave in the world: Boesmansgat (299 m)

Although Pretoria is considered the main capital, the country has **three capitals**:

Pretoria (executive), Cape Town (legislative), and Bloemfontein (judicial).

Second largest canyon in the world: Fish River canyon

SA's lowest average annual rainfall: Alexander Bay (46 mm)

NORTHERN CAPE
Size of Germany

Northern Cape = 30% of the land with around 2% of the population

<u>AND</u>

Gauteng = Less than 2% of the land with 23% of the population.

SA's longest river:
Orange River (2 090 km)

SA's largest caves:
Cango Caves

SA's highest average wind speed:
Cape Point (14.m/sec)

WESTERN CAPE
Size of Nicaragua

SA's most southerly point: Cape Aghulas

SA's highest average annual rainfall: Matiwa (2 004 mm)

LIMPOPO
Size of North Korea

SA's highest average annual maximum temperature, Lataba (35° C)

Sandton is the richest square mile in Africa, representing 9 % of the continent's GDP.

NORTH WEST
Size of Honduras

GAUTENG
Size of Kuwait

MPUMALANGA
Size of Czech Republic

FREE STATE
Size of Greece

SA's highest recorded 24-hour rainfall: St Lucia (597 mm)

St Lucia also has the largest estuarine system

KWAZULU-NATAL
Size of Portugal

LESOTHO
Size of Belgium

SA's highest peak: Mafadi (3 451 m)

Lesotho is completely surrounded by South Africa and is the highest country in the world!

Biggest dam in South Africa: Gariep dam (surface area 359 km²)

EASTERN CAPE
Size of Tunisia

SA's lowest average annual minimum temperature is 2.8° C in Buffelsfontein (now Molteno).

Highest ever recorded temperature: Dunbrody (50° C)

Lowest ever recorded temperature was - 18.6° C!

Africa's largest estuary

'iSimangaliso must be the only place on the globe where the oldest land mammal (the rhinoceros) and the world's biggest terrestrial mammal (the elephant) share an ecosystem with the world's oldest fish (the coelacanth) and the world's biggest marine mammal (the whale).' – Nelson Mandela

The name iSimangaliso means miracle and wonder.

This 332 000 hectare World Heritage Site contains eight interlinking ecosystems and three lake systems.

The area has 700-year-old fishing traditions, flocks of pelican and flamingo and one of the largest concentration of hippopotamus and crocodiles in Africa.

The coastal dunes are among the highest in the world and the 220 km of pristine beaches are the world's last significant breeding ground for the giant leatherback and loggerhead turtles.

The spectacular coral reefs support colourful underwater life making this a haven for snorkelling and underwater divers.

UNESCO

iSimangaliso Wetland Park, KwaZulu-Natal

WHEN POLITICS INTERFERES

The sanctions of the apartheid era prevented many from writing their names into the record books. In these examples, one must wonder what they would have achieved had politics been different.

Matthews Temane was a distance runner who held 17 national titles. His most impressive feat was his record-breaking half marathon in a time of 1:00:11. He came in comfortably under the then world record of 1:00:43 but due to the sporting ban, this world record was unofficial and Temane never competed internationally.

Karen Muir was the youngest world record holder in the history of organised sport. She set her first record at the age of 12. When politics prevented her from participating in the Olympics, Muir retired from swimming shortly after her 18th birthday. At the time of her retirement, she had set a total of 17 world records.

Naas Botha was the master of the drop kick and held the record for being the highest Springbok points scorer with a total of 312 points scored in 28 matches. His record was broken by Percy Montgomery. However, it took Montgomery 50 matches to score the same number of points. Imagine what record Botha could have reached had his Test career not been cut short when the IRB banned South Africa from international competition.

SPORTING ADVERSITY

MEANING: A difficult or unpleasant situation; hardships, challenges or misfortune.

IF TIMING WAS DIFFERENT

One wonders whether South Africans would have seen their country play in a home final at the 2010 FIFA world cup or seen different names on the world golfing leader boards if they had been born in a different era.

Ace Ntsoelengoe is arguably the best footballer that South Africa has ever produced. He played soccer in the '70s and '80s for both Kaizer Chiefs and the North American Soccer League. He is the only South African to be inducted into the US Soccer Hall of Fame. He has been compared to Messi, Ronaldo and Zidane.

Steve Mokone was the first Black player to play professional football in Europe when he signed with Coventry City in the '50s. He later moved to the Dutch team, Heracles Almelo, and also played for Barcelona, Valencia and Torino. He was rated one of Europe's best players, won many awards and was inducted into three different halls of fame. He was so popular he even had a Dutch street named after him and the Dutch movie, *Black Meteor,* is about his life.

Vincent Tshabalala's golfing years were turbulent. He was restrained by the South African laws which stipulated that he could not participate freely in 'White competitions' around the country. He was invited to partner with Gary Player in South Africa's World Cup team but refused to take part on political grounds. Only when the bans were finally lifted in 1975 did Tshabalala, with the help of Gary Player, compete internationally. When he did, Tshabalala went on to win the French Open. Imagine if Tshabalala had received the mentoring experienced by today's golfing leaders.

WHEN WEATHER TURNS BAD

Weather is an unpredictable factor which causes frustration and inconvenience. When the storm clouds gather, the odds seem unfairly stacked against the South African World Cup cricket team.

In 1992, South Africa returned to the international cricket arena for their first World Cup tournament. The team was one match away from creating history and winning the cup when the rain arrived. South Africa's hopes were dashed when play resumed and a revised target was calculated requiring South Africa to achieve an impossible score of 22 runs off one ball.

In 2013 South Africa's hopes of winning the Cricket World Cup on home soil were looking good but took a turn for the worse when the rain arrived. The Duckworth-Lewis method was applied to calculate the winning score and the Proteas landed up being one run short of a win and unable to proceed.

In the 2015 Cricket World Cup, the Proteas were going strong at 216/5 after 38 overs. The team was firing and looked set for a sure win before rain interrupted play. When play resumed, the targets were again adjusted by the controversial Duckworth-Lewis method and South Africa fell agonisingly short of a place in the World Cup final.

WHEN FATE INTERVENES

When fate intervenes, it can take the form of an accident or injury. For some their greatness is their destiny and written into the stars, and for others it's a sad end to a promising career.

Natalie du Toit began competing internationally at the age of 14 and had her eyes set on the Olympics. A tragic accident resulted in the loss of her left leg. A year later, she won the Commonwealth Games' Multi-Disability swimming events in world-record times. She made world history when she became the first athlete with a disability to take part in the able-bodied Olympics and was named 'Outstanding Athlete of the Games.' She was awarded the Laureus World Sports Award for Sportsperson of the Year with a Disability.

Burry Stander's story is that of a promising champion whose life was cut short when, at the age of 25, he was tragically killed by a motor vehicle whilst out cycling. At the time of his death, he had won the under-23 UCI Mountain Bike World Cup, the ABSA Cape Epic, the Singlespeed World Championships and his second World Cup title.

WHEN THE GODS HAND OUT TALENT

It is hard to imagine top sportsmen in any other role than the ones in which they are famous. So many of them are multitalented and had hard choices to make in their careers.

Herschelle Gibbs played provincial rugby, soccer and cricket and featured in South African schools' teams for all three. Most people thought he would be a rugby player until he sustained a knee injury at the age of 20 and went on to become one of South Africa's best cricketers.

Jonty Rhodes was selected for the Olympic hockey side in 1996 but was unable to play due to a hamstring injury. This forced him to concentrate on cricket - making world history by taking the most dismissals by a non-wicketkeeper in an ODI and being recognised as the best fielder in the world.

AB de Villiers must have had one of the most difficult of all career choices. His many accolades include:
- Being captain of the South Africa junior rugby team
- Shortlisted for junior national hockey and football squads
- Holding six national school swimming records
- Fastest 100 m time among South African junior sprinters
- Being a national junior Davis Cup tennis team member
- Being a national under-19 badminton champion
- Having a scratch handicap in golf
- Receiving a national medal from Nelson Mandela for a science project
- And recording his own song.

BUILDINGS TO IMPRESS

MEANINGFUL

The design of the Constitutional Court embodies the openness and transparency called for by the Constitution itself.

ARTISTIC

Street art is transforming the face of the city. From Newtown to the Maboneng Precinct, an exciting renewal is happening in Joburg's CBD.

SPIRITUAL

The Mariannhill Monastery in KwaZulu-Natal was founded by Trappist monks in 1882. Beautiful frescos adorn the cathedral ceiling and stained glass windows emit streams of light.

HIGHEST

The tallest building in South Africa and on the Continent of Africa is the 50-storey Carlton Centre in Johannesburg.

OOPSIE!

The old station in Durban was built in 1892 with a roof that can support 16 foot of snow. This was apparently the result of a mistake by the architects in London who sent the roof plans for the Toronto station to Durban. The roof in Toronto, which had been designed for the Durban climate, collapsed during the first winter.

HERITAGE

The Castle of Good Hope, erected between 1666 and 1679 by the Dutch East India Company, is the oldest building in South Africa.

ENTERTAINING

With opulent African colours and architectural features The Palace of the Lost City in Sun City is rated as one of the leading hotels in the world.

IMPRESSIVE

The spectacular buildings of Sandton are symbolic of the fact that Sandton is the richest square mile in Africa.

WEIRDEST

The home in Mpumalanga of the 'old woman who lived in a shoe' is filled with a museum and art gallery.

COLOURFUL

Music, dance, festivals - The Soweto Theatre is the cultural heartbeat of Jabulani Soweto.

MONEY, MONEY, MONEY

FROM THE DUTCH ----→ TO THE BRITISH MONARCHS ----→ TO VAN RIEBEECK ----→ TO MANDELA

The Rand comes from Witwatersrand (translated 'White Waters Ridge') the ridge upon which Johannesburg is built and where most of South Africa's gold deposits were found. When the rand debuted in 1961, it traded at R2 to the pound and 72 cents to the dollar.

1782 The Dutch Governor introduces hand-written paper money in rix dollar and stiver currency

1793 First state bank is opened

1803 Printed notes are introduced

1837 First private bank in South Africa opens

1877 First imperial bank, the Standard Bank of British South Africa Ltd, opened its doors

1882 Over 30 private banks each issue their own paper money

1961 Currency changes from pound sterling to rands with Jan van Riebeeck on the banknotes

1966 First 5 rand note is introduced

1978 A new series of banknotes are introduced, still with Jan van Riebeeck's image

THE BIG FIVE

The term 'Big Five' was coined by big-game hunters and refers to the five most difficult animals in Africa to hunt on foot. The Big Five are included on the banknotes.

RHINO

There are two species of rhino in South Africa, the Black and the White rhinoceros. Rhino's are actually neither black nor white in color, they are all grey. The white rhino's name derives from the Dutch 'weit', meaning wide, a reference to its wide, square muzzle adapted for grazing.

AFRICAN ELEPHANT

The largest land mammal in the world weighs in at 5443 kg and can be over 4 m tall at the shoulder. A bull elephant can digest about 170 kg of vegetation and drink 150 or more litres of water each day. Their rumbles can be picked up 9 km away.

Mystery Face The face that appeared on South African bank notes for many decades is Jan van Riebeeck, the commander of the first Dutch settlement at the Cape, in 1652. Historians say there are no verified images of the first settler and the South African Reserve Bank is investigating the recent debate which suggests that this is not in actual fact the face of van Riebeek.

RIX DOLLAR AND STIVER ----► POUNDS AND SHILLINGS ----► RANDS AND CENTS

1984 The R20 and R50 banknotes are introduced for the first time

1990 The R1 coin replaces the R1 banknote; notes with images of the Big Five and the country's top industries are released

1992 Coins replace the R2 and R5 banknotes

1994 The R100 and R200 banknotes are introduced for the first time

2003 The R5 coin is changed to a bimetal coin to prevent fraud

2005 Notes are changed to include all 11 official languages of South Africa

2010 The R200 banknotes are redesigned after counterfeit notes are found in circulation

2012 Banknotes bearing Nelson Mandela's image are released

AFRICAN LION

The king of the Sub-Saharan savannah is an excellent hunter although he will happily scavenge given the chance. Man, as well as a reduction in habitat and prey, has resulted in their numbers declining by 30 % in the past two decades and being placed on the IUCN threatened species list.

CAPE BUFFALO

These large animals stand 1 to 1.8 m tall and males weigh around 700 kg. Even lions don't dare take a chunk out of this beast unless they have friends helping them. When left alone they are quite placid but they are said to have killed more big game hunters than any other animal in Africa and are one of Africa's most dangerous animals.

AFRICAN LEOPARD

These shy and modest cats are nocturnal and can climb and swim and run at speeds of over 56 km per hour. A leopard's only predator is man. Man has reduced the leopards' habitat, depleted its prey and hunted it. The animal is now on the IUCN's 'near-threatened' list.

-HONOURS BOARD-

DURBAN ACCOLADES

Mercer Survey:
South African City with the Highest Quality of Life

New 7 Wonders cities:
Durban Voted One of the Seven Cities

New York Times:
#7 on the list of 52 Must-Visit Cities in the World

National Geographic:
One of the Top 10 Oceanfront Cities

Lonely Planet:
One of the Top 10 Family Beach Holiday Cities in the World

CNN:
Top 10 Underrated Cities around the World.

C40 Cities Climate Leadership Group:
Awarded Innovator City Status

CAPE TOWN ACCOLADES

New York Times:
#1 of 52 Places to Go in 2014

theguardian.com:
#1 Holiday Hotspot in Top 40 Destination Round-up

CNN:
One of world's 10 Most-loved Cities

National Geographic:
Muizenberg - One of the World's 20 Best Surf Towns

TripAdvisor:
Travellers' Choice Best Destination

Condé Nast Traveller Readers' Award:
One of the World's Top 20 Cities

Forbes.com:
One of the World's Most Beautiful Cities

Lonely Planet:
One of the World's Top 10 Party Cities

The Telegraph:
Travel Awards' Favourite City for 2013

NOBEL PRIZE WINNERS

Sydney Brenner (Physiology/Medicine)

F.W. de Klerk (Peace)

J.M. Coetzee (Literature)

Allan McLeod Cormack (Physiology/Medicine)

Albert Luthuli (Peace)

Aaron Klug (Chemistry)

Nadine Gordimer (Literature)

Nelson Mandela (Peace)

Max Theiler (Physiology/Medicine)

Desmond Tutu (Peace)

THE NATIONAL ORDERS ARE THE COUNTRY'S HIGHEST AWARDS

HONOURABLE AFFAIR

For exceptional achievement: **ORDER OF MAPUNGUBWE**

For achievements in arts, culture, and sports: **ORDER OF IKHAMANGA**

Contribution to human rights and peace: **ORDER OF LUTHULI**

For friendship to South Africa: **ORDER OF THE COMPANIONS OF O.R. TAMBO**

For distinguished service: **ORDER OF THE BAOBAB**

For courage in the face of danger: **ORDER OF MENDI FOR BRAVERY**

GRAMMY AWARD WINNERS

Ladysmith Black Mambazo (1988, 2004, 2009 and 2013) Best Traditional Folk Recording and Best Traditional World Music Album

Soweto Gospel Choir (2007 and 2008) Best Traditional World Music category

Wouter Kellerman (2015) Best New Age Album

Miriam Makeba (1965) Best Folk Music

Hugh Masekela (1968, 2012) Nominated for Best World Music category

Lebohang 'Lebo M' Morake (1995) Best Instrumental arrangement with accompanying vocal

ACADEMY AWARDS

Gavin Hood's *Tsotsi* (2005) Best Foreign Film

Charlize Theron (2004) Best Actress, *Monster*

Darrell Roodt's *Yesterday* (2004) Nominated for Best Foreign Language Film Category

Searching for Sugarman (2013) Best Documentary Feature

Caiphus Semenya (1985) Nominated for Best Original Music Score, *The Color Purple*

Jonas Gwangwa (1987) Nominated for Best Original Music Score, *Cry Freedom*

Ordinary Love (2014) Nominated for Best Music Originial Song, inspired by Nelson Mandela

Invictus (2010) Morgan Freeman and Matt Damon were nominated for their roles playing Nelson Mandela and Francois Pienaar respectively

Soweto Gospel Choir (2009) Became the first South African artist/group to perform at the Academy Awards

THE SOWETO GOSPEL CHOIR

DAY OF RECONCILIATION

In the days before democracy, South Africa commemorated two separate occasions on this day:

The Afrikaners remembered the day when the Voortrekkers defeated Dingane's Zulu army at the Battle of Blood River in 1838. After the killing of their leader Piet Retief and the massacre of many of their people, the Voortrekkers took a solemn vow that if God helped them to defeat the Zulus, they would build a church and keep the day sacred for all generations. During the battle a group of roughly 470 Voortrekkers defeated a force of more than 10 000 Zulu. Only three Voortrekkers were wounded and some 3 000 Zulu warriors died in the battle.

The African National Congress (ANC) activists remembered this day in 1961 when they launched Umkhonto we Sizwe, the party's military wing, with the purpose of overthrowing the apartheid government. Umkhonto we Sizwe is Zulu for 'Spear of the Nation' and became the armed wing of the ANC. It was co-founded by Nelson Mandela in the wake of the Sharpeville massacre. Its founding represented the conviction that the ANC could no longer limit itself to nonviolent protest and its mission was to fight against the South African government.

Today the Day of Reconciliation is an official public holiday on which South Africans, instead of focusing on previous conflict, put the past behind them and celebrate the achievement of democracy. The people work towards building bridges and creating a peaceful nation. South Africans celebrate their harmony and recommit to continued reconciliation and nation building with an emphasis on equality, mutual respect and a shared future.

South Africa's different population groups:

• African •

Africans, also referred to as Blacks, are in the majority at just over 41 million, making up 79.2 % of the total population. The African population is made up of four broad groupings: The Nguni, comprising the Zulu, Xhosa, Ndebele and Swazi people; the Sotho-Tswana, who include the Southern, Northern and Western Sotho (Tswana people); the Tsonga and the Venda.

• Coloured •

There are 4.61 million Coloured people, a number which makes up 8.9 % of the population. Although this group is officially recognised as such, the name 'Coloured' has become contentious. These are a people of mixed lineage descended from slaves brought to the country from East and Central Africa, the indigenous Khoisan who lived in the Cape at the time, indigenous Africans and Whites. The majority speak Afrikaans.

• Indian •

This group is also referred to as Asian and their population stands at 1.28 million, representing 2.5 % of the total population. A majority of this group are Indian in origin but there is also a significant group of Chinese South Africans. Many of the Indians are descendants of the indentured workers who were brought to work on the sugar plantations of what was then Natal in the 19th century. The majority are largely English-speaking, although many also retain the languages of their origins.

• White •

There are 4.58 million Whites, a number which makes up 8.9 % of the population. This group is made up of mainly Afrikaners, who were descendants of the Dutch, German and French Huguenots who came to the country from the 17th century onwards, and the English-speakers, who were descendants of settlers from the British Isles who came to the country from the late 18th century onwards. Other immigrants and descendants of immigrants from the rest of Europe, including Greeks, Portuguese, Eastern European Jews, Hungarians and Germans make up the rest of the White population.

Source: Census 2011

Natural Disasters

South Africa is susceptible to a number of extreme weather events with the most common being floods, droughts, fires and large storms.

While floods have resulted in the highest economic cost of damages (approximately R 18.7 billion), droughts have affected a larger proportion of the country's population. The total cost of weather-related disasters between 2000 and 2009 is estimated to be approximately R 9.2 billion. The economic losses from weather-related disasters in South Africa between 1900 and 2014 is in the region of R 50.7 billion.

DROUGHT - The 1991/1992 drought is ranked as the worst natural disaster in South Africa causing the failure of around 70 % of crops. This, in turn, led to farm closures, increased debt and labour layoffs. Direct job losses were estimated to be 50 000 while a further 20 000 jobs were lost in related sectors. The Reserve Bank reported that the loss of GDP during the 1992 drought was approximately 1.8 % (R 6000 million).

FLOODS - KwaZulu-Natal was devastated by Tropical Cyclone Domoina in 1984, and in 2007 and 2008 the damage to coastal property and infrastructure as a result of storm surges was estimated at R 1 billion. It was, however, the 1987 flooding in KwaZulu-Natal that is recorded as the country's worst. The storm washed away 14 bridges and caused severe damage to thousands of kilometres of road. Approximately 68 000 people were left homeless and 388 people were killed. In SA, between 1980 and 2009, on average 35 people died annually due to large flooding disasters – this figure excludes the deaths in flash flood events not officially declared as disasters.

WILD FIRE - Fires are a frequent occurrence, particularly in the eastern part of the country which has a long dry season lasting for up to five months. In 2002, fires in Mpumalanga destroyed 24 000 ha of pasture and left four people dead, with damages amounting to more than R 32 million. Between 2007 and 2008 KwaZulu-Natal and Mpumalanga experienced fires that resulted in huge loss of revenue - about R 5 160 million. As much as 61 700 ha of plantation forest was burnt, equating to 2.9 % and 9.5 % of the total area of plantations in these two provinces respectively. ForestrySA gauged the value of standing timber burnt to be R 1.33 billion.

Climate change is expected to increase the frequency and extent of extreme weather events, which will increase the risk of disasters, particularly for vulnerable areas. Southern Africa is widely recognised as one of the regions most vulnerable to climate change.

Photo: Ansie Vahrmeijer
Sandstorm at Bainsvlei, Bloemfontein, on 16 October 2014.

LIGHTNING - South Africa's Highveld region as well as the areas surrounding Lesotho produce amongst the highest lightning strikes per square km/annum in the world. In South Africa the annual fatality rate due to lightning strikes is estimated to be more than 260, about three times as high as in the USA.

EARTHQUAKES - While most South Africans will remember the Johannesburg earthquake of 2014 measuring 4.6 on the Richter Scale, it was in 1969 that the biggest recorded earthquake occurred in the town of Tulbagh. It measured 6.5 on the Richter scale and caused rock falls and fires.

HAIL - Hailstones the size of coconuts were reported to have fallen during a devastating hailstorm in 1936 in Gauteng killing more than 26 people. In 1949, in Pretoria West, hailstones with a circumference of 23 cm broke 12 000 large windows at the Iscor (now Mittal Steel South Africa) plant in the area, and damaged hundreds of cars at the plant.

SNOW - In September 1981 Johannesburgers were surprised by a spring blanket of snow over the city. A similarly unusual snowstorm occurred in the same month 45 years earlier (1936).

BARRY HILTON on braaing...

South Africans love their braais, especially the boertjie. But when a boertjie asks me for a braai I say no. You have to say no. When he says 'Wil jy braai? Kom, môre gaan ons braai' (Do you want to braai? Come tomorrow, we're going to braai). I have to say no because I like to eat before 11. If he says 'Ons gaan nou nou braai – Ja ons gaan nou nou braai' (we're going to braai now now) even if you want to say yes, you hesitate because you know what he is actually saying is 'We will braai now now, after the 12 bottles of brandy.' Then when you go there the next day, you know boertjies don't eat anything but meat. You know you're going to graze only meat, no salads. So you arrive and you're starving because you haven't eaten all day. You knock on the door and the boertjie opens the door and says 'Hallo, ons gaan nou braai.' He offers you a doppie 'met eish'. By seven o' clock you're getting peckish so you go into the kitchen to check if the dogs have left anything. By nine o' clock the boertjie is seriously 'klapping' his Klippies and Coke and he says 'Nou nou gaan ons braai.' By 10 o' clock you're visually showing signs of malnutrition and your face looks like your bum is busy eating your liver. It's getting hard to breathe and it dawns on the guy that you are hungry. He tells you not to worry 'Moenie worry nie, nou gaan ons braai!' Then he calls to his wife 'Vrou take the meat out the deep freeze.'

www.barryhilton.co.za

"THE COUNTRY'S FUNNIEST" SHARE WITH US about LIFE IN SOUTH AFRICA

KEVIN PERKINS ON LIFE IN SA...

In South Africa people only have to have their groceries go bad in their fridge ONCE from the genius concept of Load Shedding to get GATVOL. When the chips are down, we stand together shoulder to shoulder, we put up with situations that would make the average POM's head spin! No water? Can't bath or shower? No problem - grab the lux and a towel and head out to the pool. Chatting to your neighbour's wife while standing kaalgat (naked) on the top step of the pool has become a new social taboo. Bath time is private - avert your eyes people! No electricity ...build a generator from an old tractor and some scoobie wire ...don't know the words to Nkosi Sikelele ...NO PROBLEM ...just sing the bits you know LOUDER. As the problems cascade over us thick and fast and threaten to destroy the foundation of our society ...we make a plan ...we devise solutions and most South Africans (NOT in government) will work together in the most laudable, cooperative way.

www.kevinperkins.co.za

Many things have changed in South Africa including our road names. Botha Avenue is now Buthelezi's Avenue. Jan Smuts is Smuts Ngonyama and Tony Leon has become Tony Yengeni. On my way to the airport recently, I followed Yengeni, into Ramaposa Road which is the e-toll that runs past the bank and ends up outside parliament. By now I was lost. Then I saw a big fancy new road in the distance. The sign read 'Jacob Zuma Boulevard'. Jacob Zuma Boulevard is a long downhill that runs all the way to Nkandla. In fact, if you are with Zuma you can put your Mercedes in neutral and freewheel all the way! I stuck with Zuma for ages but made sure I jumped off before he became Robert Mugabe. Then I saw Mandela on my right - Winnie not Nelson. Nelson's the old road. I followed Winnie, which is uphill with potholes so deep you lose reception on your cell phone, and then went right into Musi Maimane Mews. Musi is a one-way street so you have to go right. He changed direction a lot, did a U-turn and crossed Zuma, then turned again and double-crossed Zuma. It was all too confusing. I don't use a GPS. For 50 years we had White ladies telling us what to do so I don't want another instructing me to 'Turn right now'. For my next trip to the airport, I am taking Julius Malema. At least that way you can bypass Jacob Zuma altogether. Eventually I was so lost I asked a White man for directions. I should have asked him in the beginning. After all, which middle-aged White South African doesn't know the quickest way out of the country?

www.benvoss.co.za

DIANS

The thing about White South Africans is that they take being punctual so seriously. White people are never late for anything. Let's say myself and a White colleague are flying to Durban (King Shaka International Airport) from OR Tambo International Airport (Johannesburg). We all know we need to be at the airport an hour before departure. A White South African will be at the airport four hours before departure. Why, why, why? I will tell you why. It is to make us look bad as Black people. Who in their right mind goes to the airport four hours before their plane takes off? White people, that's who! If you don't believe what I am talking about, when last did you see a relaxed Black guy at the airport? We are always running because we are about to miss our plane. White people are at the airport early just in case. In case a truck overturns on the freeway on the way to the airport or, in case their flight is cancelled, White people need time to change flights. Another thing about Black people is that, before we even think of leaving our houses for the airport, we need to first visit our friends and families in Soweto, Alexandra, Thembisa, Kagiso and Vosloorus. And when I am going to Durban, I need to visit my friends and families to collect all the orders for 'sea water' from the Indian Ocean. Yes, 20 litres of sea water for Soweto and 10 litres for Alexandra. Because as a Black person, you dare not go to Durban if you don't bring home the 'sea water.'

Cheers!

Although South Africans are known for being enthusiastic beer and wine drinkers, their indulgences stretch to other tipples as well. As with the country's food, South Africa's drinks have been influenced by its history, rich culture and colonial past.

WHITE LIGHTNING

The Americans call it 'moonshine', to the warm-blooded Irish it is 'poteen' and the Swiss know it as 'kirsch'. In South Africa it is 'witblits' in the Cape and for those in the northern parts of the country, it is just 'mampoer'. This uniquely South African, strong, homemade, distilled brandy is made from fruit using recipes that have been passed down from generation to generation.

The legend of mampoer is so entangled in South African folklore that it is difficult to distinguish between fact and fable. It is alleged that General Joubert's men probably obtained this liquor from Mampuru, a Pedi chief, hence the origination of the liquor's name. Chief Mampuru, who instigated the murder of his half-brother, Sekoekoenie, is thought to have distilled mampoer from the plentiful maroelas in the area.

The test to determine the quality is very simple: Pour a small quantity on a flat surface and light it. If it all burns off with a clear blue flame, it is unadulterated and full strength. Not for the faint-hearted, it is guaranteed to take your breath away with each sip. This practice has led to mampoer and witblits (which literally means 'white lightning'), also being called 'fire water'.

The farmers in the Marico district (North West Province), where mampoer distilling is part of everyday life, have to sell their mampoer discreetly - mampoer distilling for retail sale is still illegal. This goes back to 1924 when the government passed a law giving KWV a monopoly on brandy production. All stills had to be marked and registered with Customs and Excise, and detailed records kept as to the amount and strength of any liquor produced. Mampoer has long ago become part of South Africa's cultural heritage. To the people who distil and drink 'mampoer', it has become a way of life.

NON-ALCOHOLIC FAVOURITE

For a refreshing, thirst-quenching alternative to overly sweet sodas try a Rock Shandy. This South African favourite is made with half lemonade (or Sprite), half soda water, a dash of Angostura bitters, a slice of lemon and lots of ice.

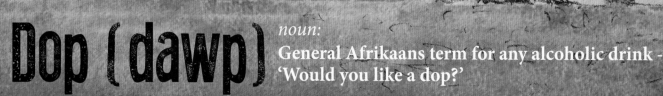

Dop (dawp)

noun:
**General Afrikaans term for any alcoholic drink -
'Would you like a dop?'**

Van der Hum liqueur was distilled for centuries by South African women before it was bottled officially. This wonderfully aromatic liqueur is a blend of brandy, wine, naartjie (mandarin oranges/satsumas) peel and spices. The drink is named after the Dutch Admiral Van der Hum who is said to have been 'fond of it to the point of distraction.'

BRANDY – BIGGEST AND BEST

The KWV Brandy Cellar is said to be the largest distillery of its kind in the world, with 120 pot stills under one roof.

KWV took the title of Best Brandy and Cognac Producer in the World at the 2015 International Spirit Challenge (ISC). It was the first time in the ISC's 20-year history that a brandy and not a cognac had won the award.

AMARULA – The Spirit of Africa

This world-famous local cream liqueur is exported to more than 100 countries across the world. Winner of three different international competitions, the results are consistent and speak to the universal appreciation of this African Original. The golds were awarded by the International Wine and Spirit Competition (IWSC) in London, at the Concours Mondial in Brussels, and at the San Francisco World Spirits Competition.

The fruits of the marula tree are a favourite of elephants, baboons and monkeys who are said to get drunk and party on these fermenting, overripe fruits. The sacred marula tree is the source of fascinating legends. In Swaziland the annual Marula Festival is celebrated at the king's royal residence. In keeping with the belief that the marula is a fruit fit for kings, each household presents the king and queen mother with a portion of the brew they have made, before partaking of the drink themselves.

Known as a 'Marriage Tree' amongst the Zulu, the marula tree is believed to bestow vigour and fertility on those who marry beneath its branches. Tribal wedding ceremonies are held in its shade. The hard stones inside the fruit are often dried and strung together in a necklace that traditionally symbolises love. Marula trees are dioecious which means they are either male or female and the Venda people believe that to determine the gender of an unborn child, if a woman wants a son she should drink the bark infusions of the male tree and for a daughter, the female tree. If the child of the opposite gender is born, the child is said to be very special for its ability to defy the spirits.

My South Africa is an article which epitomises the actions and feelings of everyday South Africans. It was written by Professor Jonathan Jansen, a modern-day icon of democracy. As rector of the University of the Free State, Professor Jansen has earned a formidable reputation for transformation and for a deep commitment to reconciliation in communities living with the heritage of apartheid. He is the author of many books and, as an educationalist, holds an impressive collection of degrees and awards, including the position as President of the South African Institute of Race Relations. *My South Africa* went viral shortly after it was released.

MY SOUTH AFRICA

My South Africa is the working-class man who called from the airport to return my wallet without a cent missing. It is the white woman who put all three of her domestic worker's children through the same school that her own child attended. It is the politician in one of our rural provinces, Mpumalanga, who returned his salary to the government as a statement that standing with the poor had to be more than just a few words. It is the teacher who worked after school hours every day during the public sector strike to ensure her children did not miss out on learning.

XYZ

My South Africa is the first-year university student in Bloemfontein who took all the gifts she received for her birthday and donated them - with the permission of the givers - to a home for children in an Aids village. It is the people hurt by racist acts who find it in their hearts to publicly forgive the perpetrators. It is the group of farmers in Paarl who started a top school for the children of farm workers to ensure they got the best education possible while their parents toiled in the vineyards. It is the farmer's wife in Viljoenskroon who created an education and training centre for the wives of farm labourers so that they could gain the advanced skills required to operate accredited early-learning centres for their own and other children.

My South Africa is that **little White boy** at a decent school in the Eastern Cape who decided to teach the Black boys in the community to **play cricket**, and to fit them all out with the togs required to play the gentleman's game. It is the two **Black street children** in Durban, caught on camera, who put their **spare change** in the condensed milk tin of a white beggar. It is the Johannesburg **pastor** who opened up his church as a place of shelter for illegal immigrants. It is the **Afrikaner woman** from Boksburg who nailed the White guy who shot and killed one of South Africa's greatest **freedom fighters** outside his home.

My South Africa is the quiet, dignified, determined **township mother** from Langa who straightened her back during the years of oppression and decided that her struggle was to **raise decent children**, insist that they **learn**, and ensure that they not succumb to bitterness or defeat in the face of overwhelming odds. It is the **two young girls** who walked 20kms to school everyday, even through their matric years, and passed well enough to be accepted into **university studies**. It is the student who takes on **three jobs**, during the evenings and on weekends, to find ways of paying for his university studies.

My South Africa is the teenager in a wheelchair who works in townships serving the poor. It is the pastor of a Kenilworth church whose parishioners were slaughtered, who visits the killers and asks them for **forgiveness** because he was a beneficiary of apartheid. It is the **politician** who resigns on conscientious grounds, giving up **status and salary** because of an objection in principle to a social policy of her political party. It is the young **lawman** who decides to **dedicate his life** to representing those who cannot afford to pay for legal services.

My South Africa is the man who went to **prison for 27 years** and came out embracing his captors, thereby releasing them from their impending misery. It is the activist priest who dived into a crowd of angry people to **rescue a woman** from a sure necklacing. It is the **former police chief** who fell to his knees to wash the feet of Mamelodi women whose sons disappeared on his watch; it is the women who **forgave** him in his act of contrition. It is the Cape Town university **psychologist** who interviewed the 'Prime Evil' in Pretoria Centre and came away with emotional attachment, even **empathy**, for the human being who did such terrible things under apartheid.

My South Africa is not the angry, corrupt, violent country whose deeds fill the front pages of newspapers and the lead-in items on the seven-o'-clock news. It is the South Africa often **unseen**, yet powered by the **remarkable lives** of ordinary people. It is the **citizens** who keep the country together through **millions of acts of daily kindness**.

The uKhahlamba

To the Zulu it's uKhahlamba,
meaning 'barrier of spears'.
To the Afrikaans it's Drakensberge,
meaning 'dragon mountains'.

**To locals it's simply
'The Berg'.**

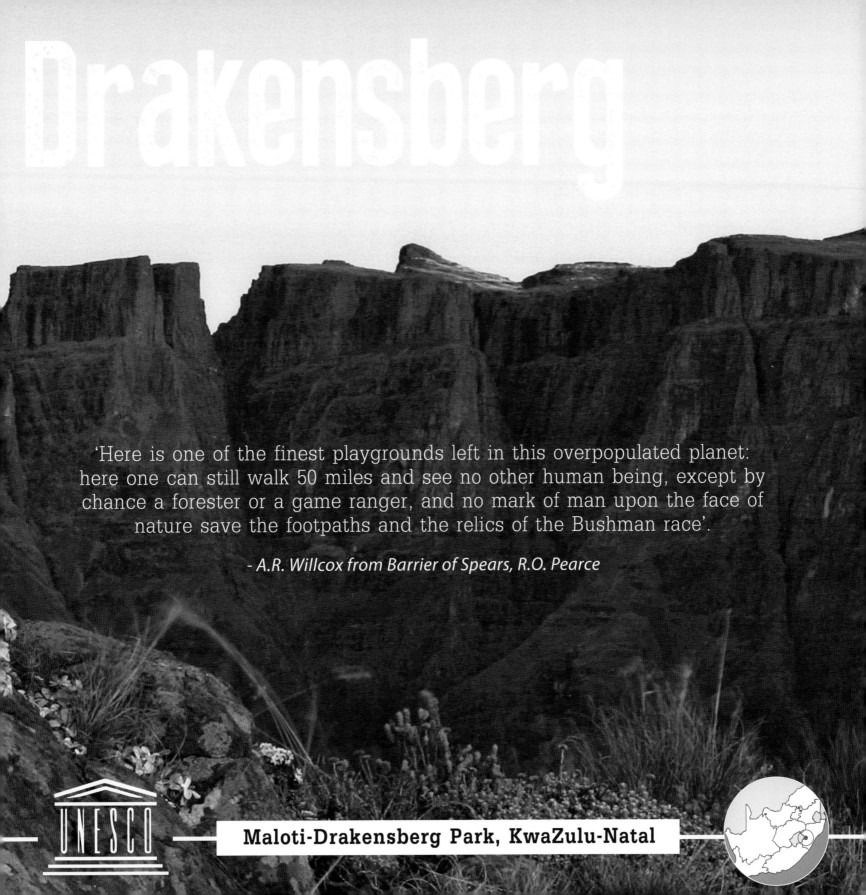

Drakensberg

'Here is one of the finest playgrounds left in this overpopulated planet: here one can still walk 50 miles and see no other human being, except by chance a forester or a game ranger, and no mark of man upon the face of nature save the footpaths and the relics of the Bushman race'.

- A.R. Willcox from Barrier of Spears, R.O. Pearce

UNESCO

Maloti-Drakensberg Park, KwaZulu-Natal

Rugby players use designated words to call the line-out formation. The Natal team used words which start with a letter. Rugby captain, Wynand Claassen, caused much confusion when he played the formation which used a word designated with a 'U'. The Afrikaans player could not understand why his team-mates were not responding appropriately to his call of 'ONION'.

The City Oval cricket ground in Pietermaritzburg is the only first-class cricket ground in the world with a tree within the boundary. You get a four for hitting the tree, a six for clearing the tree and if you take five wickets in an international game, then you have the honour of planting your own tree at the ground.

Morné du Plessis captained the SA rugby team in test matches. He definitely inherited his sporting genes from his family. His father captained the SA rugby team, his mother captained the SA women's hockey team and his uncle Horace Smethurst captained the SA football team.

During the marriage ceremony of Orlando Pirates player, Jomo Sono, the player got word that his team was 2-0 down. He left the wedding reception, arrived at the match at half time in a tuxedo with soccer boots. He scored a hat trick and Pirates won the semi-final of the BP Challenge cup 4-2.

Onion Confusion   Mind the Tree   A Family Affair   Jomo Cosmos Wedding

Breaking a Leg – literally   Swimming Affair   Who Needs Astroturf

SOURCE: David O'Sullivan and Kevin McCallum, *The Penguin Book of South African SPORTS trivia.*

Fanie Lombard was a single-leg amputee. At the Paralympics in Sydney in 2000, he twisted his 'only' ankle whilst warming up for the long jump. However he proceeded to participate and when doing the javelin he broke his 'other' leg. With help from technicians and their tools, he managed to repair his prosthetic leg in time to win gold and set a new world record.

Springbok test rugby player, Jaco Reinach, also held the South African 400 m record in athletics so completing an iron man should have been an easy feat. However he could not swim. Reinach used water wings for the swim which developed a leak and resulted in the athlete having to be rescued to prevent him from drowning.

The infamous Sun City Golf Course, which is built in the SA bushveld, is the home of the Million Dollar golf tournament. The story goes that Sol Kerzner was most concerned about the dry golf course. Seeing the desserts at dinner, he got the idea to use green food colouring. In his efforts to make the course look good for the opening in 1979, Sol Kerzner sent a team with sprays of green food dye to colour the surrounding rough.

At the age of 13, golfer Retief Goosen was playing off a three handicap and had already had his first of many holes-in-one. However, when he was 15, whilst playing on Pietersburg golf course, he was struck by lightning which burnt the clothes from his body and melted his watch into his wrist. It was a miracle he survived. He was back on the golf course a few weeks later and went on to become a South African golfing legend. Amongst many accolades Goosen is lauded for having finished first on the PGA and European Tour seven and fourteen times respectively and has won the US Open Championship twice.

AB de Villiers was the opening batsman in the SA game against Australia. He made sure he had an early night so he would be fresh for the 10 am start. He got rather a fright when his alarm woke him at 10.30. In a panic he dressed and ran into the hotel dining room for breakfast only to find the dinner still being cleared. His alarm had gone off mistakenly at 10.30 pm.

SPORTS TRIVIA

Goose Lightning

AB on AM and PM

Eat your Words

A Grassy Eyeball

The Springbokken are Born

Before the South Africa game against England at Newlands in 1996, Jack Bannister said that he would eat the piece of paper he was holding if SA won the series against England. He did so afterwards on a live television broadcast.

When the Lions played the Springboks in 1974, a scuffle broke out between the players which resulted in one of the players calling for the game to be halted so that they could look for the glass eye of Springbok Johannes de Bruyn. When the eye was found he popped it back into his eye socket. He was later presented with a trophy of a wooden rugby ball with a glass eye mounted on top.

The sister of South African athletes, Piet and Philip J Blignaut, decided to embroider a springbok on their hunting vests which the brothers then used when competing in an athletic competition in England. They met Paul Roos who thought this was a great idea. Roos was appointed captain of the rugby team and, when embarking on the team's first-ever tour of England in 1906, Roos advised the media to call them 'De Springbokken'. *The Daily Mail* published the name 'Springboks' and so the legacy began. At this time the country was just recovering from the conflict of the Boer War. On accepting the captaincy, Roos stated 'I would like to make absolutely clear at the outset we are not English speaking or Afrikaans speaking, but a band of happy South Africans'.

DIAMONDS

The first diamond (appropriately named Eureka) was discovered near the Orange River in 1866. South Africa has mined almost 10 % of the total world production of diamonds. In 1880 Cecil John Rhodes helped found the De Beers Mining Company which soon controlled the entire country's diamond industry. Today it is the world's largest producer and distributor of diamonds.

- The biggest man-made hole in the world -
Kimberley or Jagersfontein?

← The size of each man-made hole →
in comparison to Table Mountain

KIMBERLEY

The Kimberley hole is renowned as the biggest hand-dug hole in the world. In 1914 the hole was 240 m deep and 470 m wide and it has a surface area of 17 ha. The hole was dug by hand by 50 000 miners and is one of South Africa's top tourist attractions. It produced 14.5 million carats of diamonds before closing down in 1914.

JAGERSFONTEIN

The surface hole of Jagersfontein mine measures 19.65 ha and it reaches a depth of 275 m. There is much debate around at what depth the horse-powered machinery took over, however, the mounting evidence suggests that Jagersfontein is, in actual fact, the deepest hand-dug hole in the world. The mine produced 9.52 million carats of diamonds before officially closing around 1969.

10.5 cm

Energi
139 kcal
7%*

Actual size

THE CULLINAN DIAMOND

Discovered in 1905 near Pretoria, this is the largest rough diamond ever found. Almost the size of a Coke can, it weighed 3 106.75 carats (621.35 g). The stone was cut into nine major stones and 96 smaller stones, the largest of which is set in the head of the British monarch's royal sceptre and kept in the Tower of London.

THE EXCELSIOR

The Excelsior diamond was discovered by a miner at the Jagersfontein Mine in 1893. It weighed 971.5 carats. Interestingly, until the discovery of the Cullinan diamond in 1905, the Excelsior was the world's largest known uncut diamond. It was shipped to London and valued by experts at amounts ranging wildly from £50 000 to £500 000. For his honesty in handing over this massive find, the miner was rewarded with £500 and given a horse equipped with a saddle and a bridle.

RECORD PRICED BLUE DIAMOND

A 122.52 carat blue diamond was discovered at Cullinan Mine in 2014. Blue diamonds are more valuable than their white counterparts and Cullinan is renowned as the world's most important source of blue diamonds. This latest exceptional discovery could fetch a record price. So far the highest price on record paid for a rough diamond was $35.3 million in 2010. This stone is expected to break that record.

LARGEST KNOWN VIVID PINK DIAMOND

Almost the size of a bottle cap, this 59.6 carat pink diamond is known as the Pink Star. It is twice the size of any vivid pink diamond ever brought to auction. It was mined in South Africa in 1999 as a 132.5 carat rough by De Beers and was sold on auction for $83.2 million to Diamond cutter Isaac Wolf. Wolf reckons its worth at least $150 million.

CENTENARY DIAMOND

The Centenary Diamond is the largest modern fancy cut diamond in the world and is insured for $100 million. At 273.85 carats this was the third largest uncut diamond produced by De Beer's Premier Mine. It was classified as D level - the highest grade of a diamond that is colourless and flawless both internally and externally.

South Africa has so many inventions to be proud of such as Pratley Putty, which has been to the moon and the Dolosse that protect our shoreline. More recent inventions continue to create world firsts.

The country's reputation for leading the way in medical research was enhanced by the invention of the CAT scan and Dr Christiaan Barnard, who made world history with the first heart transplant. Today South Africa continues to lead the way with cutting-edge research and innovation.

The uMkomaas Pedestrian Bridge

This pre-stressed ribbon bridge received a Fulton Award for Design Aspects in 2007. At the time it was the first of its kind in Africa and the longest in the world, with a clear span of 150 m.

INVENTION INNOVATION

Portable Braai

The Cryoprobe

A pencil-shaped device with a frozen tip used for eye surgery. It is famous for treating ex-President Nelson Mandela for eye cataracts the day after he was sworn into office. Afterwards, Mandela was able to read a speech at the United Nations without spectacles.

Teabag Water Filter

Scientists at Stellenbosch University in the Cape have tackled the human rights issue of how to provide clean, cheap drinking water to those most in need. The research produced a point-of-use filtration system using nano-sized fibres that not only destroy bacteria but also prevent bugs from attaching themselves to the surface of fibres. The research is of consequence to the one-billion-plus people who die every year from water-related ailments.

ADEPT 320T

In a world first, a Durban aviation company used digital technology to develop a light aircraft engine that weighs less than a conventional piston engine, is more fuel efficient, and can run on a variety of fuels. The engine won the Autodesk International Inventor of the Year Award in 2008, the SABS Design Excellence Award in 2010 and the SABS Chairman's Award for Design Excellence in 2011.

Commercial Fly Farm

This world first was established in Cape Town. The flies are reared on a very large scale to lay eggs that are hatched into larvae on organic waste material. Instead of polluting the environment with abattoir and other organic waste, the waste is turned into high-quality protein that can naturally replace fishmeal in industrial farming. This also helps save our seas. Every ton of MagMeal (insect-based protein meal) produced from existing waste, is a ton of fish that doesn't need to be taken from our seas.

Thin Solar Cells

A micro-thin metallic film was created at the University of Johannesburg. This technology has made solar electricity five times cheaper than the previously used solar photovoltaic cells, making solar power a more affordable and infinitely more environmentally friendly option than coal.

Oil-Can Guitar

An engineer and avid guitarist wanted to make silly tin guitars to sell for cheap souvenirs. Their popularity grew particularly since top South African jazz musician Jimmy Dludlu incorporated them into his concerts. Even UB40 has bought and used some! Call it the 'Afri-can guitar!'

DIY African Foosball

Outdoor Snooker Table

INSPIRATION
INTRIGUE

Power-free Foetal Heart Monitor

This portable and extremely useful device, developed by a Cape Town paediatrician and team , uses ultrasound to measure a baby's heart rate during labour, scanning the womb and taking printable 'pictures' of the foetus. Interestingly, the device employs wind-up power, solar power, rechargeable batteries or mains power, and can be used anywhere.

Astraphobe

Produced in 2015 the Astraphobe protects electronics from surges created by lightning. Unlike other surge protectors, the Astraphobe knows when a storm is coming. Instead of diverting high voltages to the ground, it disconnects the line completely, preventing any surges reaching your equipment.

Antiretroviral Microbicidal Gel

Researchers at the Centre for AIDS Programme of Research in South Africa received a standing ovation at the 2010 International AIDS Society Conference when they announced that the use of an antiretroviral microbicidal gel can protect against HIV transmission. Mathematical modelling suggests that, in South Africa alone, this gel can prevent up to 1.3 million new infections and 8000 HIV-related deaths during the next 20 years.

Penile Transplant

South African doctors at Stellenbosch University successfully performed the world's first penis transplant in 2015 on a 21-year-old man whose organ had been amputated three years ago after a botched circumcision. The success of the transplant was celebrated within months when the patient not only had a full recovery and full urinary and reproductive functions but announced to the world that he was to become a father.

Garden Spray

In the old days, before candles

...South Africa had electricity.

Page courtesy of loadshedding

Could it be true?

To some these myths are appealing fireside stories, to others merely fantasy. However, through the years the accumulated evidence raises interest even amongst the most cynical. It's up to you to decide... Could they be true?

Chinese Explorers

According to author Gavin Menzies, the largest fleet the world had ever seen, sailed from its base in China on the 8th of March 1421. With huge ships 127 m (417 ft) long and 52 m (171 ft) wide and built from the finest teak, the fleet was dispatched by the Emperor Zheng 'to proceed all the way to the end of the Earth to collect tributes from the barbarians beyond the seas' and unite the whole world in Confucian harmony. The journey would last over two years and circle the globe. When they returned, however, Emperor Zheng had lost control and China went into a long period of self-imposed isolation, but not before their very accurate maps (and the presence of longitude) had spread to the West.

It was also recorded by the first Dutch settlers that on their arrival they had met locals with a lighter skin than the indigenous Khoikhoi that lived in the Cape. These locals had oriental features and a markedly different speech. We don't know for sure whether the massive Chinese fleet ever sailed past the Cape of Good Hope, but the map of Africa, even with its imperfections, tells us that they must have known something about the continent.

Black Jews

The origin of the so-called 'Black Jews' has been an ongoing mystery for many years. The Lemba people, who number around 70 000 to 80 000 people, live in the far northern Limpopo Province as well as in Zimbabwe. They claim they are the descendants from a lost tribe of Israel and direct descendants of the Queen of Sheba in her union with King Solomon of the Bible. Some families have Middle Eastern names and their language contains non-Bantu words. Their belief systems are different to the traditional Bantu belief systems: they observe the Shabbat and their tombstones bear the Star of David.

It wasn't until recent genetic analysis was conducted that the sceptics were silenced. Genetic tests carried out by British scientists have revealed that many of the Lemba tribesmen in Southern Africa do, in fact, have Jewish origins.

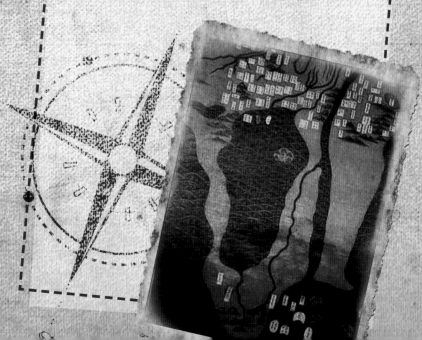

Phoenician Wreck

It is believed that the area from False Bay across the Cape Flats to Table Bay was once covered by the Sea. The land from Cape Point towards Cape Town was therefore, at some point, an island. In fact a complete skeleton was exposed in a Maitland Quarry near Cape Town. The skeleton was identified by Dr Leonard Gill of the South African Museum as that of a rorqual whale. Maitland is a considerable distance from the current coastline so it appears that there has been a rise in the level of the Cape Flats.

Furthermore, the timbers of old ships have been dug up from the sands of the Cape Flats on several occasions in the past. The Phoenicians flourished over 3000 years ago at about the same time as the Egyptian pharaohs and the founding Hebrews of the Middle East were active. The circumnavigation of Africa by the Phoenician explorers, 600 years before Christ, was described by the Ancient Greek historian Herodotus. He suggests that the the Egyptian King Necho had sent out a fleet manned by a Phoenician crew with orders to sail west.

Reports of a Phoenician wreck in Cape Town were first attested by George Thompson in 1827 when he came across timber deeply embedded in sand. In 1852 Charles Bell examined an exposed wreck which appeared to be part of a vessel in excess of 70 ft in length. The vessel had been raised hundreds of feet up above the high-water mark over 15 km from the sea. In the 1880s construction workmen who were digging in the Maitland area of Cape Town uncovered a vessel. The timber, which smelt like Cedar wood, burnt exceptionally well so it was sold off as firewood. In fact, there was so much wood that it took months before the entire ship was excavated, chopped up and sent to Cape Town for sale.

Many years later in 1924 the evidence was investigated. Two elderly men who had helped dig up the ship years before were interviewed and recalled seeing the mast of a ship, which was in excess of three feet (almost a metre) in diameter and over 180 ft (54 m length). Is it possible that the wreck excavated from the Maitland area belonged to the ancient Phoenecians from a time when the sea covered the Cape Flats?

Africa's Heartbeat

Drumming is Africa's heartbeat. There is also the familiar term 'The Bush Telegraph' which is linked to the phenomenon that people can interpret messages from the beat of a drum. Roger Webster, in his book *The Fireside Stories*, shares many tales about the way in which messages were communicated throughout Africa with drums. He relates how the news of Queen Victoria's death in 1901 was sent: 'The news was cabled to West Africa, and those who were there say that the drums started beating in relays which went on for days; in the remotest areas the tribespeople were talking about the death of the Great White Queen.'

Another such example is the sinking of the *SS Mendi*, the troopship that sank in the English Channel in 1917 while carrying hundreds of Black South African volunteer troops. According to Webster's research, the drums started beating out a message and the women and loved ones in the remotest villages of KwaZulu-Natal started wailing, for they knew that their men had died. The government telegraph officially confirming this terrible tragedy only reached Durban three days after the women had begun their mourning.

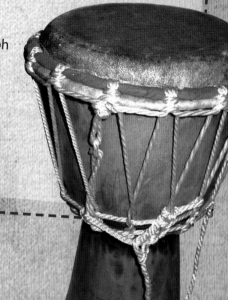

'The only man I envy is the man who has not yet been to Africa...

for he has so much to look forward to.'

– source unknown

WHAT'S YOUR FAVOURITE?

MOOI

SA'S FAVOURITE
ASK AFRICA FOOD BRANDS SURVEY

- All Gold
- KFC
- Coca-Cola
- Huletts Sugar
- Albany Bread
- Tastic
- Nulaid eggs
- Danone
- Mugg & Bean
- Rajah spices
- Koo Baked Beans
- Robertsons spices
- Black Cat Peanut Butter
- McCain frozen vegetables

nom... nom...

YUM!

202

REMEMBER THESE
TV ADVERTS

SANTAM - What a country - hippo-crossings, car guards and load shedding!

LUNCH BAR - What kind of Mac are you? (speaking to Makatini)

FARMER BROWN - They taste so good 'cos they eat so good

BLACK CAT - Black Belt Huh? No, Black Cat!

CASTLE LAGER - I bless the rains down in Africa

MELROSE CHEESE - Oh boy! Mom remembered Melrose!

OMO - Oooh Eh Eh - Just one small cap is enough!

REDRO - I call everything I love Wedwo

CREMORA - It's not inside... It's on top!

CASTROL - Ja Boet!

National SYMBOLS

It is crucial that South Africa's natural national symbols, which include three animals and two plants, be protected.

A country's symbols – seal, motto, flag, anthem, coat of arms and natural symbols – tell its story and play a crucial role in building pride and a sense of belonging. South Africa's national symbols are rich in heritage, and tell the stories of the country's abundant natural and cultural diversity.

Department of Arts and Culture,
South African Government Online

National animal: Springbuck/springbok
(Antidorcas marsupialis), Lize-Marié Dreyer 2012

SOUTH AFRICA
STANDARD POSTAGE

NATIONAL ANIMAL

The Springbok (Afrikaans: 'spring' means jump and 'bok' means buck or antelope) is the only true gazelle found south of the Zambezi and is the fastest antelope. Measuring up to only 75cm in height, these small animals can leap up 4 m high and 15 m in length and can run as fast as 90 km per hour.

A national symbol of South Africa under white minority rule, the name 'Springboks' was to be replaced by 'Proteas' across all sporting teams when the ANC government came into power. However, the rugby team retained the name Springboks after Nelson Mandela allowed it as a gesture of goodwill to the mainly white (and largely Afrikaner) rugby supporters. What an honour for our rugby players to be associated with the athletic Springbok! Once roaming in their hundreds of thousands in the arid regions of southern Africa, the small herds today are found only in protected areas and farms.

National flower: Giant or king protea
(Protea cynaroides), Lize-Marié Dreyer 2012

SOUTH AFRICA STANDARD POSTAGE

NATIONAL FLOWER

If the bulky rugby players have a small gazelle as their symbol, the national cricket team has the giant or king protea (Protea cynaroides) as theirs. Despite also being found outside South Africa, the king protea is clearly associated with the country and in particular with the beautiful fynbos of the Cape Floral Kingdom. It is one of the most spectacular members of the Proteaceae family, lending credibility to its choice as our country's national flower. The pink-coloured flowers are arranged in the shape of a large artichoke (Cynara).

Although mostly found in the Western Cape, the king protea still occurs throughout large parts of the country and is, therefore, listed as 'of Least Concern' on the South African Interim Red Data list.

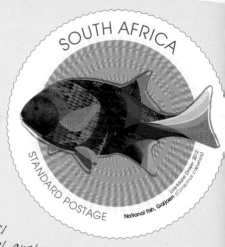

NATIONAL FISH

The galjoen (*Dichistius capensis*) is found only in Southern African waters, from the Namibian coast in the west to the coast of KwaZulu-Natal in the east. Due to its endemism, the galjoen was nominated as our national fish by the late Margaret Smith, former Director of the J.L.B. Smith Institute of Ichthyology in Grahamstown. 'Galjoen' is the Dutch for 'galleon' and it is believed that the fish got this name from the early Dutch settlers who thought that the line of markings along the fish's body looked like the gun ports on galleons.

Due to overfishing, the galjoen is now listed as Red by SASSI (Southern African Sustainable Seafood Initiative). Recreational anglers may only catch two galjoen (minimum size 35 cm) per day between 1 March and 14 October each year. They are not allowed to sell their catch.

NATIONAL TREE

The real yellowwood (*Podocarpus latifolius*), South Africa's national tree, is a broad-leaved evergreen tree species that grows up to 40 m in height and is not only among the tallest trees in the world but is also the oldest. Podocarpaceae is a small cone-bearing family, which, along with the indigenous cedars, represents the small number of coniferous tree species indigenous to South Africa.

Timber from the real yellowwood was used in the old Cape homestead as flooring. It was also used to make beautiful furniture and as railway sleepers, wagon boxes, coffins and butcher blocks. In the past the yellowwood was so sought after for its timber that from being an abundant resource, it is almost extinct in some areas. All the species of Podocarpus are now protected in South Africa.

NATIONAL BIRD

Almost never seen outside the country, the blue crane (*Anthropoides paradisea*) is South Africa's national bird. This tall, ground-dwelling bird stands a little over a metre high and is pale blue-grey in colour with a white crown, a pink bill, and long, dark grey wingtip feathers which trail to the ground.

The blue crane is a bird very special to the amaXhosa, who call it indwe. They say when a man distinguished himself by deeds of valour, or any form of meritorious conduct, he was often decorated by a chief by being presented with the feathers of this bird.

Due to habitat loss and deliberate or accidental poisoning, this elegant bird began a sudden population decline from around 1980 and is now classified as critically endangered.

WHAT KIDS SAY...

South Africa has the best schools 'cause we have such nice teachers.

– Nathan, age 7

What do you like about South Africa?

They have Lego shops and make movies!

– Daniel, age 7

Soccer!

– Eli, age 5

...because I like to play rugby 'cause I tackle someone.

– Jesse, age 3

It's warm and everybody be good and we have lots of friends to keep us company.

– Emily, age 6

...we are all made differently. We have Zulus, Christians and Indians. We all look very different.

– Sphesihle, age 7

We are called the rainbow nation because...

...after apartheid Black people and White people came together and made a rainbow nation.

– Gabriel, age 11

...there are not only one kind of people here, we have lots.

– Ethan, age 9

...we have lots of rainbows! Especially in Westlake.

– Abigail, age 9

Running in an open space, like a field.

— Maddelena, age 7

To be yourself, nobody is holding you down.

— Goodnews, age 8

What does it mean to be free?

To be free is to be yourself, not to be anybody else.

— Mekael, age 8

No one troubles you and you don't have a little space, you have a lot of space.

— Vedha, age 6

There's so many... all the animals, all the different kinds of sport and the lots of trees.

— Cooper, age 8

...that we are in Africa and are quite hot.

— Bhavya, age 6.

...the cars that we drive.

— Neha, age 7

My favourite thing about South Africa is ...

...the beaches.

— Megan, age 7

...nature, all the types of animals we have.

— Cruz, age 7

International Inspiration
TAKING THE WORLD BY STORM

From humble beginnings to international acclaim, these South Africans have taken the world by storm and inspired millions!

Photo © Glenn Francis, www.PacificProDigital.com

· Nomvimbi & Nana Meriwether ·

The founder of Meticulous Tours, Nomvimbi Meriwether, began her life as a missionary conducting refugee programmes along the Kruger Park Area. She is now owner of Meticulous Tours travel agency in Washington DC and the co-founder of a multimillion-dollar health and basic education charity in Southern Africa, the Meriwether Foundation. Her fundraising clout in the US enjoyed a major boost when her daughter, Soweto-born Nana Meriwether, won the Miss USA crown.

Pam Golding

Pam Golding is founder and life president of the globally recognised Pam Golding Property group, a multi-million Rand business with 300 branches, 186 franchises and a staff of around 3000 across the world. In recent years, Golding has also become a global networker and facilitator, promoting SA and its investment opportunities. She was named Lifetime Achiever at the Ernst & Young World Entrepreneurship Awards (2009), and is a founding member of Proudly South African and the International Women's Forum.

Photo © Martin Schmitt

· Trevor Noah ·

Trevor Noah has been profiled in *Rolling Stone*, *Newsweek*, *The Wall Street Journal*, and CNN. Noah's one-man show *The Racist* at the 2012 Edinburgh Fringe was a sold-out run that became one of the most talked about shows at the Festival. Born in South Africa in 1984 to an African mother and a Swiss father, Noah's mixed family was illegal under the laws of apartheid. Trevor Noah continues to tour all over the world where he performs in front of large audiences and is the host of the American Award-winning *The Daily Show* on Comedy Central.

· Mark Shuttleworth ·

As the first South African in space, Shuttleworth has inspired people the world over with his tenacity and brilliant business acumen. Born in Welkom in the Free State, he showed promise from an early age as head boy in primary and high school. He went on to study at the University of Cape Town and in 1996, whilst still a student, he founded Thawte, an Internet commerce security company which he sold for $ 575 million. Since then he has set up a venture-capital company HBD ('Here Be Dragons' named after the uncharted territory on early maps). He also founded the Shuttleworth Foundation, a non-profit organisation supporting innovation in education in Africa. He is currently worth around $ 500 million.

Patrick Soon-Shiong

This son of Chinese immigrants is the world's richest doctor with a net worth of almost R 150 billion.

Born in 1952 Soon-Shiong grew up as a Coloured in Port Elizabeth after his parents fled from China. He finished high school at the age of 16 and received his medical degree from the University of the Witwatersrand. After an internship at the Johannesburg General Hospital he moved to Canada, then to the USA. Soon-Shiong became well known for transplanting pancreas cells to treat diabetes and he invented ground-breaking treatment delivery technology for breast cancer. He founded two drug companies, Abraxis and American Pharmaceutical Partners, which he sold for R 112 billion and he holds 50 US patents, including that of blockbuster pancreatic cancer drug Abraxane. Forbes ranks Soon-Shiong's fortune among the 100 largest in the US.

· Elon Musk ·

A full-blown maverick of all things business, Elon Musk has invented, engineered and invested. As the founder and CEO of various enterprises, his largest claim to fame is as one of the co-founders of PayPal. This Pretoria-educated entrepreneur created and sold his first video game at the age of 12. He left South Africa in 1988 at the age of 17 and by 2015 his net worth was estimated at $ 12.7 billion and he is now regularly compared to great inventors such as Thomas Edison and Henry Ford. Some have called him the next Steve Jobs. His latest battery technology invention is anticipated to change the way the world and the environment see energy.

· Dave Matthews ·

Hailing from Johannesburg where he attended St Stithians College, Dave Matthews was recently named the US's most successful touring act of the decade and is reportedly worth R 2 billion!

Sol Kerzner

Sol Kerzner grew up in the poor suburbs of Johannesburg before building Sun City. He then went on to become one of the world's biggest hotel magnates. He built two man-made lakes, four hotels and two Gary Player designed golf courses within 10 years. He then expanded with mega-casino hotels in the Bahamas, Connecticut and Atlantic City. The launching party of Atlantis Resort in Dubai is recognised as one of the biggest parties that have ever been held in the history of the world and The Atlantis Resort and Casino in the South China Sea is estimated to be worth $ 1.5 billion.

Bernie Wolfsdorf

This South African moved to Boston at the age of 24. He has been named the most highly rated immigration lawyer worldwide by the peer-reviewed International 'Who's Who' of Business Lawyers.

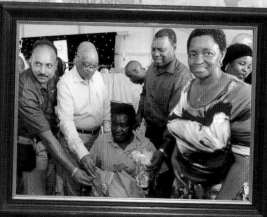

· Kumi Naidoo ·

This South African human rights activist was executive director of the international environmentalist group Greenpeace. After his own apartheid experiences in the 1970s and 1980s, Kumi Naidoo led global campaigns to end poverty and protect human rights.

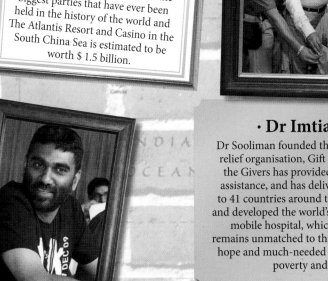

· Dr Imtiaz Sooliman ·

Dr Sooliman founded the non-governmental disaster-relief organisation, Gift of the Givers, in 1992. Gift of the Givers has provided food, supplies and medical assistance, and has delivered over R 1.2 billion in aid to 41 countries around the world. They have designed and developed the world's first and largest containerised mobile hospital, which is the best in Europe and remains unmatched to this day. Gift of the Givers brings hope and much-needed relief to areas affected by war, poverty and natural disasters.

THE 67 BLANKETS FOR NELSON MANDELA DAY

A Guinness World record was set when the gardens of the Union Buildings were covered with 3 133 m² of blankets. The blankets, which were crocheted and knitted by South Africans and other supporters around the world, were distributed across all nine provinces to people in need.

SOUTH AFRICA IS A NATION OF GIVERS.
A survey revealed that:

93 % OF PEOPLE SUPPORT CHARITIES AND SOCIAL CAUSES.

54 % donate money, 31 % give food or goods, 17 % volunteer time.

Source: State of Social Giving series, commissioned by the Centre for Civil Society, National Development Agency and SA Grantmakers' Association.

a NATION THAT cares

Oxford Dictionary Definition: **Eish:** South African informal exclamation used to express surprise, annoyance, pain, etc.

Eish!
Hard day in Africa.

Photo courtesy © Bianca Preusker

'You are the Rainbow People of God'.

The term 'rainbow nation' was coined by Archbishop Desmond Tutu. The colours of the rainbow capture South Africa's diverse races, tribes, creeds, languages and landscapes. The rainbow is symbolic of hope, promise and reconciliation.

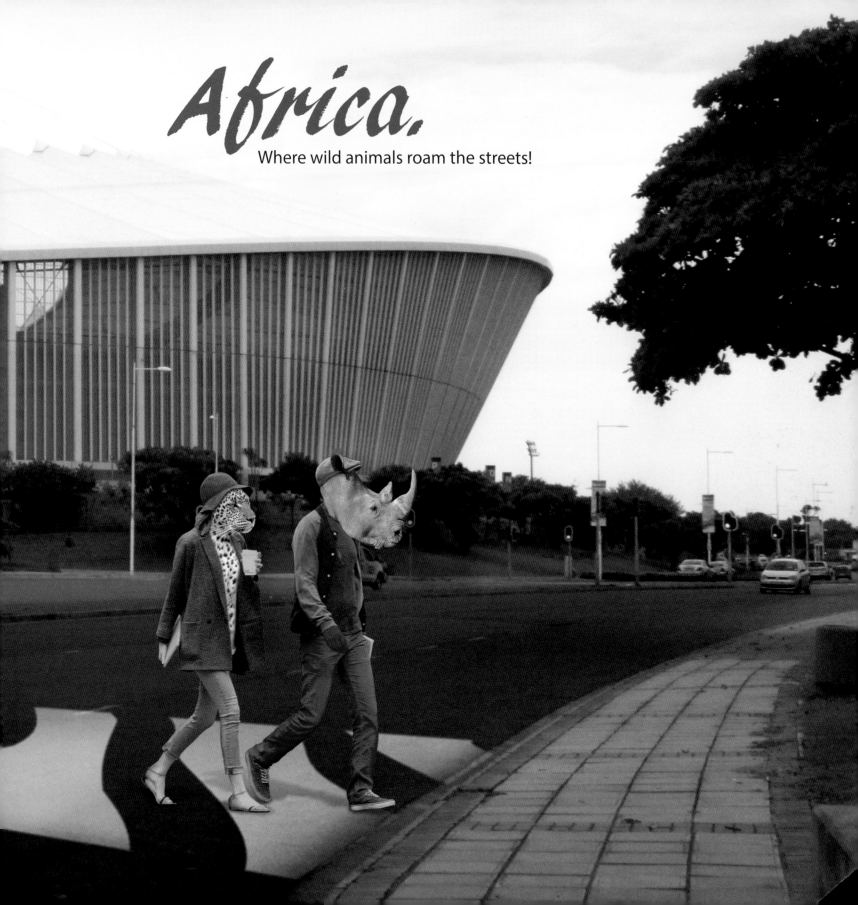

Africa.

Where wild animals roam the streets!

REFERENCES

The information sourced for the book was not taken from academic records or encyclopaedias, but rather from the vast array of interesting and informative non-fiction books which are available in South African bookstores and libraries, as well as reliable and comprehensive websites. The information presented in the book represents the tip of the iceberg and readers will find any one of the books listed entertaining and enjoyable. They come highly recommended!

ABOUT SOUTH AFRICA

Dawid van Lill. *See South Africa Visual Facts*. Human & Rousseau.

Bill Malkin. *It's a Fact*. Jonathan Ball Publishers.

South Africa Yearbook 2008/2009. www.gcis.co.za

JP Landman. *The Long View*. Jacana.

Allan Jackson. *Facts About Durban*. FAD Publishing.

WTF What the Fact. MapStudio.

Ann Gadd. *Things ewe never kn'ewe about South African place names*. MapStudio.

CULTURE, QUOTATIONS AND PROVERBS

Jennifer Crwys-Williams. *The Penguin Dictionary of South African Quotations*. Penguin Books.

Julia Stewart. *Stewart's Quotable Africa* and *Stewart's Quotable African Women*. Penguin Books.

Dianne Stewart. *Wisdom from Africa*. Struik Publishers.

HISTORY

Roger Webster. *At the Fireside Series*. Spearhead.

Max du Preez. *Of warriors, lovers and prophets* and *Of tricksters, tyrants and turncoats*. Zebra Press.

Francis Wilson. *Dinosaurs, Diamonds & Democracy*. Umuzi

Peter Joyce. *100 Moments That Mattered - Events That Built South Africa*. Zebra Press.

Alexander Parker. *50 People Who Stuffed Up South Africa*. Two Dogs.

Alexander Parker. *50 Flippen Brilliant South Africans*. Jacana.

Ben Maclennan. *Apartheid The Lighter Side*. Chameleon Press.

ON THE LIGHTER SIDE

Sarah Britten. *The Art of the South African Insult*. 30° South Publishers.

Jill Ritchie. *Ag Shame!* Papillon Press.

SPORT

Peter Joyce. *100 Memorable Sporting Moments*. Zebra Press.

David O'Sullivan. *The Penguin Book of South African Sports Trivia*. Penguin Books.

WEBSITES

The websites which were used extensively and are of particular interest are listed below. The full list of website references is available on request from the publishers.

www.southafrica.info
www.sahistory.org.za
www.sagoodnews.co.za
www.thesouthafrican.com
www.leadsa.co.za
whc.unesco.org
www.nelsonmandela.org
www.oxforddictionaries.com
www.economist.com
www.statssa.gov.za
www.environment.gov.za
Facebook - Africa, this is why I live here

This book is dedicated to South Africa's future.....
- To those who believe in it,
- To those who are a part of it,
- And to those who are determined
  to positively improve it.

We would love to receive your feedback and welcome your comments.
For more information on the book and how it can be personalised
as a gift for events and companies:

Email
info@awesomesa.co.za

Visit our website
www.awesomesouthafrica.co.za

Phone
+27 (0)82 786 8450